Ingenhoven
Overdiek
und Partner

High-Rise
RWE AG Essen

**Ingenhoven
Overdiek
und Partner**

**High-Rise
RWE AG Essen**

Edited by
Till Briegleb

With contributions from
Lothar Baumgarten
Ulrich Behr
Werner Blaser
Till Briegleb
Klaus Daniels
Michael Dickson
Klaus Frankenheim
Fritz Gartner
Heinrich Hacke
Dieter Henze
Winfried Heussler
Christoph Ingenhoven
Klaus Klein
Lars Leitner
Richard Long
Tony McLaughlin
Achim Nagel
Dieter Schweer
Lothar Stempniewski
Joachim Stoll
Clemens Tropp
Klaus-Dieter Weiß
Ulrich Werning

Birkhäuser Publishers
Basel · Boston · Berlin

Kindly supported by:
Hochtief AG, Buro Happold, HL Technik AG, Werning Tropp und Partner, Josef Gartner & Co., ADO-Roste GmbH, Carpet Concept, FSB – Franz Schneider Brakel GmbH, Siteco Beleuchtungstechnische GmbH

Editor Till Briegleb
Editorial Till Briegleb, Jan Esche
Documentation Petra Pieres
Design Beate Tebartz, Stephanie Westmeyer
Translation from German into English Tobias Kommerell, London

A CIP catalogue record for this book is available from the Library of Congress, Washington D.C., USA

Deutsche Bibliothek Cataloging-in-Publication Data
High-rise RWE AG Essen / Ingenhoven Overdiek und Partner. Hrsg. von Till Briegleb. With contributions by Ulrich Behr ... - Basel ; Boston ; Berlin : Birkhäuser, 2000
  Dt. Ausg. u.d.T.: Hochhaus RWE AG Essen
  ISBN 3-7643-6108-5

This work is subject to copyright. All rights are reserved, whether the whole or part of the material is concerned, specifically the rights of translation, reprinting, re-use of illustrations, recitation, broadcasting, reproduction on microfilms or in other ways, and storage in data banks. For any kind of use, permission of the copyright owner must be obtained.

© 2000 Ingenhoven Overdiek und Partner, Düsseldorf, und Birkhäuser – Publishers for Architecture, P.O.Box 133, CH-4010 Basel, Switzerland
Font: Rotis SemiSans
Printed on acid-free paper produced from chlorine-free pulp. TCF ∞

Printed in Germany
ISBN 3-7643-6108-5

9 8 7 6 5 4 3 2 1

Contents

8	Prefaces	Werner Blaser Martin Pawley
10	Introduction	Till Briegleb
18	Interview	Christoph Ingenhoven in Conversation with Klaus-Dieter Weiß
32	Tour	
52	Support Structures	Michael Dickson
54	Construction	Lothar Stempniewski and Heinrich Hacke
62	Façades	Ulrich Behr, Fritz Gartner and Winfried Heussler
74	Engineering Concept	Tony McLaughlin
76	Air	Joachim Stoll
80	Facility Management	Klaus Daniels and Dieter Henze
86	Lighting	Ulrich Werning and Clemens Tropp
88	Models	Till Briegleb, Christoph Ingenhoven and Klaus Frankenheim
96	Garden	Till Briegleb, Christoph Ingenhoven and Klaus Klein
102	Project History	Achim Nagel and Lars Leitner
110	Interior	Till Briegleb
116	Hoofbeats	Lothar Baumgarten
118	Neandertal Line	Richard Long
120	Design	Achim Nagel
126	User	Dieter Schweer
130	Technical Data	
132	Team	
136	Acknowledgements	
138	Illustrations	
139	Bibliography	
140	Authors	

Prefaces

Werner Blaser

The dissolution of mass into zero gravity, the seamless merging with the atmosphere, an architectural language that unfolds before our eyes, discreet, calm and entirely unpretentious, the glass sheath that allows nature to be experienced, a contemplative quality, the spectacle of nature that turns into a permanent internal sensual experience, this light architecture conjuring up openness and transparency, perhaps even a vulnerability of the form.

Martin Pawley

The sun beams down on the Ruhr city of Essen. From the top of the silver RWE tower the flat landscape of North Rhine Westphalia stretches as far as the eye can see. A silver blimp makes its way across the sky. Down below a silver BMW glints in the sun. Silver is the colour of German racing cars, the colour of advanced technology, and the colour of the building that lays claim to be Europe's first ecological high rise.

The events that brought this building into existence date back to the summer of 1991 when the results of two international architectural competitions were announced. Ingenhoven Overdiek und Partner came second in the contest to design the Commerzbank tower in Frankfurt, but first in the contest to design the new headquarters building for the RWE nuclear power to waste management group in Essen. In the end it was the smaller 30-storey RWE tower that was completed first, with a sky garden on its roof, a fully-breathing double facade and super transparent white glass to maximise daylighting.

Christoph Ingenhoven, the firm's principal, believes that it is important for architects today to design more than just the aesthetic form of a building. 'The challenge is to make the architecture responsible for the internal climate', he says. 'And to achieve that control through the building envelope and not through energy consuming mechanical climate controls.'

That is where the celebrated 'fishmouth' detail designed for the RWE Tower comes in. Unobtrusively serving every storey of the building, in one sense it is simply part of the cladding, but it took exhaustive wind tunnel testing and miniaturising industrial design before it could be put into production. Now, like the skin of a living creature, it works by itself, helping to stabilise the internal climate without consuming energy.

The completion of this building in 1997 marked a milestone in the development and expansion of modern architecture. Today Ingenhoven Overdiek und Partner has an elite team capable of brainstorming tomorrow's design challenges with the same inspiration, energy, and elegance.

Introduction
Till Briegleb

The new corporate headquarters for the RWE AG in Essen by Ingenhoven Overdiek und Partner is a prototype. To conceive the world's first ecological high-rise building represents an impressive pioneering achievement – to create a prototype for a completely new kind of building, however, requires the application of exemplary principles and the courage to innovate; in short: it requires complete reformation.

The manifestation of architectural reformation is illustrated by the impact of societal interaction on architecture. Furthermore, architectural reformation has always unreservedly endorsed a democratic stance and the notion of free communication. To illustrate this point, let us examine religious architecture: the opulent stage set of a Catholic mass forced the congregation into a role of voiceless humility with an overwhelming display of architectural magnificence and cultic splendour as a drastic reminder to the faithful of their utter irrelevance. However, by shifting the focus back to the essence of faith, the schism brought about a radical change in the manner churches were built. The architectural expression of the new Protestant world view – lack of decorative abundance, reduced and clear structures and restrained colours – allowed the people to resume their place at the centre of religious life. While before everything revolved around the dominion and the one-sided and exclusionary communication of the church, the reformation churches created a restrained backdrop for the faithful that elevated the congregation to the part of protagonist.

The same reflex is manifested in the modernist response to the architecture of the Kaiserreich. The hierarchical building structure informed by imperial self-confidence, in which every person was assigned a place related to the role they fulfilled, and the presence of supremacy was immodestly demonstrated through size and décor, underwent a dramatic reduction. The desired equality of all people was expressed through unrestricted spaces, reproducible modules, transparency, neutrality and a total lack of stucco features, in an attempt to de-throne architectural status symbolism. As far as architects were concerned, this structure was meant to evoke exchange rather than obedience; but that dream – like all dreams – did not carry any tangible truth at its surface and therefore it too required to be reformed during its voyage through history.

Postmodernism and deconstructivism in turn created another 'Catholic' structure, often inadvertently, where the aesthetic genius attempted to triumph over people's lives; the problem of a hierarchical perspective reappeared. Instead of conceiving a building that revolved around the requirements of its users, the people represented nothing more than actors in an opera in the eyes of its composer, the artist/architect. There are dramatic buildings in which not even a cupboard could be placed because the bizarre dynamics of the building's design lacked any regard for practical considerations; these buildings may be an exception, but the reaction of a new generation of architects who picked up the vocabulary of the 1920s on a new level and are therefore collectively known as 'secondary modernists', shows that there is, in fact, a strong desire by society to recapture the notion of the 'serviceable sovereignty' of architecture as a counter-concept to pomp and circumstance.

For the logically consistent application of the notion of serviceable sovereignty the RWE office tower merits the status of prototype, because this building's code is based on user-logic. All investigations conducted by the architects centred around the question of what a person could require of a building in which he/she will spend a third of their lifetime. One would think that this is standard practice for architects, but considering the way most buildings have been conceived it is evident that only the most dedicated architects are able to pursue this principle from planning stage to completion, and only under more or less perfect conditions.

In the RWE project, the two main players had the same objectives. Christoph Ingenhoven – designer of the office tower and proponent of user-requirement-oriented high-quality building – and the RWE board – the client, eager to underline the transformation of their enterprise from monolithic energy corporation to modern service provider with a grand architectural gesture – were the ideal team-mates for this ambitious project. Money was not a problem and even the architect's simple premise – 'The central issue of all our planning ideas is the well-being, even the happiness of the people who will occupy this building' – was not allowed to evaporate during the planning process.

The fact that such simple attitudes nonetheless require enormous efforts, energy and invention may initially come as a surprise, but to put these notions into practice one needs to stick to the rules of life: the creation of freedom and liberty requires the creation of clever solutions rather than bowing to conventions.

This journey begins with urban planning and continues, after many years, into an open-ended process, as this kind of design concept has reverberations that go be-yond handing over the keys. Long after completion, Christoph Ingenhoven and his team continued to work on the building, be this regarding artwork, the maintenance of the gardens or the selection of suitable brochure racks in the lobby; the architects were determined to prevent countless mini-revolts to counteract the concept they had fought for with such vigour and conviction. The problem is this: the users' very individual requirements often do not go hand in hand with the overall design concept. Sticking pictures onto the external glass walls, filling every conceivable nook and cranny with flower pots or installing zigzag railings in the gardens and pronouncing them 'a piece of art' – these urges, detectable among the entire RWE workforce, illustrate

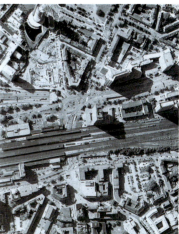

This aerial photograph from 1999 shows the integration of the RWE tower into the urban structure south of Essen central station.

clearly how an architects' educational efforts in matters of taste are usually deleted by the users' sense of individuality. The old problem facing modern architecture will always remain: is it permissible to have chintz and floral prints in a strictly formalised glass building? The perils inherent in a strictly defined architectural concept with its minutely detailed permutations are due to the sheer magnitude of its conclusiveness, especially if the fundamental reasoning behind it is to provide the ideal conditions for a living environment rather than creating an artificial or artistic illusion of one.

This endogenous perspective, in which beauty is borne out of the harmonious employment of the 'serviceable' aspects of architecture – this being one of Ingenhoven's maxims – led the architects to produce a 'high-rise fault list', because only when inadequacies of past solutions have been analysed is it possible to develop a new solution in order to achieve a state of utter contentment – both technically and aesthetically.

And this 'fault list' is long and substantial, not least because the client's desire for social and public representation in a high-rise building has hitherto usually prevented a close examination of the real advantages this type of building actually has. This is why countless tall boxes, sealed from the outside world and consuming vast amounts of energy, have appeared all over the world, making their occupants sick, not happy.

'The things we wanted to achieve were quite simple', says Ingenhoven as he describes the initial planning process, 'because we thought it absurd that in a high-rise building you need electric light during the day, that inadequate sun protection causes a permanent thunderstorm-ambiance, that you can't open the windows or that in order to talk to a colleague in the office on the next floor up you have to go on a 200-metre trek'. The fact that the inherent advantages of a high-rise building, such as unrestricted daylight and fresh air supply and high density, were completely reversed in most previous office towers by installing elaborate, expensive and energy-wasting air conditioning and lighting systems and non-sensical office configurations, must have positively fired the inventiveness of the young architect (Ingenhoven was only 31 at the beginning of the planning process). In order to delete all the points on the fault list of the autistic giants known as office towers, several issues needed to be addressed: the need for unhealthy air conditioning had to be reduced as much as possible, the offices were not to shut out the outside world and should be fully integrated into the building's internal life, the need for technical equipment had to be minimised through the optimised use of natural light and natural energy sources (active and passive) and the building had to be logically and effectively linked to its urban environment.

Instead of indulging in detailed aesthetic exercises and trend-related design fantasies the Düsseldorf architects concentrated on the benefits of industrial modular production. 'Big buildings have big potential' is Christoph Ingenhoven's reply when asked what fascinates him about high-rise buildings. 'Thanks to the industrialised and compressed form of a high-rise building we can scrutinise the details more intensively.' The façade element, for example, can be produced in high numbers thanks to a very detailed and meticulous design process that was necessary to develop a standard element suitable for industrial manufacture. The architects even extended the efficient principle of modular reproduction to the building's structure and equipment.

But the vital system component in the creation of a building that was not conventionally representative (of the client's/occupant's social position) but representative and functional, was the double-layer glass façade. Developed over many years of planning and testing in co-operation with façade specialist Gartner, it almost completely avoids the problem of wind pressure on the windows in the internal glass layer so that the natural contact to the outside world is guaranteed, even on the 30th floor: for a breath of fresh air, just open the window. The sun screens, situated in the space between the two glass membranes, protect office workers from overexposure to sunlight while still providing sufficient daylight, without causing heat build-up. The use of solar energy and maximum daylight access thanks to a 100%-glazed façade minimise the need for additional energy sources. The façade, the absorptive concrete ceilings collectively make up the building's naturally balanced and extremely energy-efficient cooling and heating system.

Finally, the fully glazed façade not only allows the outside and inside worlds to interact, it also provides an external layer of communication: life within the RWE headquarters becomes as much part of city life as the sky's reflections on the façade, lending the tower a perpetually changing appearance, which is particularly effective when observed from the Opernplatz.

Ranging from a warm amber glow to a cool platinum sheen – reflecting the sun's position or the general weather conditions – the tower is sheathed in various shades of the most beautiful and the cheapest of all building materials: daylight. As dusk approaches, this effect is intensified until it gradually blends into a nocturnal x-ray aesthetic. Once it is dark, the lights inside lend the tower the appearance of a magnificent back-lit étagère; viewed from the outside, the hustle and bustle in the offices is transformed into a three-dimensional dramatisation of daily corporate business; and its proximity to the Alvar Aalto theatre incorporates the RWE tower's architecture into an opera of busy civic life. Thanks to the flood-lit whirlpools in the basins in front of the tower this temple of work is dressed in light even after office hours. The flittering reflections of light reach beyond the baldachin hovering above the water, all the way to the upper floors

where the light patterns are in turn reflected in the ceilings, lending the façade yet another, almost romantic face.

In order to illustrate the architect's fundamentally humane approach we must point out the long bench underneath the loggia. No-one had asked Ingenhoven to provide any resting facilities at this junction of public and corporate life. But the voluntary inclusion of a small place that is welcoming and inviting, where the fountain's gentle platter and an interesting urban view towards the opera invite passers-by to sit down for a while, beautifully illustrates Christoph Ingenhoven and his partners' sensitivity and social competence. Christoph Ingenhoven once said, '…if I had not been able to comply with the needs and requirements of the people who live and work in this city, I would not have done this project' – a categorical statement that resonates throughout the building, making its presence felt for every passer-by and even for those not particularly concerned with architecture. The appearance of the gleaming cylinder, a symbol of technological reasoning and classic aesthetics, is simple, straightforward and logical.

Although Christoph Ingenhoven is a reformed modernist through and through, with the design for this tower he stuck to the 100-year-old formula by Louis Sullivans which states that a skyscraper requires the same main ingredients as a Greek column: a base, a shaft and a capital.

The dynamically cone-shaped base is only visible from the garden because the rising terrain towards the entrance area at the front conceals the base completely. The facilities that could not have been adequately accommodated within the relatively slim shaft have been placed behind the wide cockpit-like window on ground floor level: the casino, restaurant and conference rooms. The inclined frustum-shaped window front, which necessitated various different shapes of window panes, creates a link between the lunchtime office workers and the garden and lake in front of the tower. The elegant landscaping devised by Christoph Ingenhoven and landscape architect Klaus Klein is, metaphorically speaking, brought into the building. The large, semi-circular canteen with its opulent glass front exudes the sublime restraint that is encountered throughout the building.

The rear viewing platform and the entrance with driveway and loggia on the front of the tower serve as a termination to the base, forming a level where the tower is firmly anchored in all its power and elegance. Like a piston out of a cylinder the tower emerges from the pale and smooth canteen roof that is clad in the same natural Bergell stone as the lobby. Viewed from inside, the boundaries between inside and outside become blurred and the sensation of interior space is extended beyond the building itself. This enhances one of the entrance area's specific features: a transparency that makes you forget that there's an office tower rising above this delicate structure.

By placing the services cores and elevator shafts not in the centre but at the building's perimeter, Ingenhoven Overdiek und Partner were able to design a spacious lobby that invites the confusing association of the tower standing on only a few columns and a cushion of glass and air. The high-quality and subtle materials (architectural concrete, natural stone, wood and glass) used in the uncluttered and serene lobby reveal the restraint of the entire design concept as soon as one enters the building. Superior understatement combined with an ambiance of good taste and unobtrusive presence define the character of transformed classicism that defines this building.

In the lobby, the architect's philosophy is articulated in many ways: by the curved stairs cutting into the floor at a sharp angle and the symmetrically arranged space above; by the indirectly lit, so-called 'Porsche wheel' the ceiling that transmits central stresses onto the columns and, above all, the virtually unrestricted view through the building towards the city. Inviting rather than intimidating, neutral where necessary and elegant where possible – the lobby stimulates the senses, it avoids opulence and cosiness, it demonstrates the power of a functional and open-minded aesthetic that is not concerned with intimidation, exclusion or seclusion. In short, it is the perfect portal for a modern service industry enterprise.

The fact that this ambiance continues throughout the building is due to the ability of Ingenhoven Overdiek und Partner to compose the building in the manner of a fugue. The recurring theme of technical classicism appears in various forms and interpretations but is never lost in a haze of improvisations or stylisation. Very much in the manner of Bach's method of composition, the musical mathematics of the building's architecture always remain close to the principles of serviceable sovereignty. As a result, Christoph Ingenhoven's architecture does not indulge in luxurious self-aggrandizement but simply aims to provide all the vital prerequisites for a dignified and human working environment. In contrast to conventional office towers – dark caves lined with carpet and veneer creating an artificial climate – the optimised minimalism of the RWE tower provides a veritable comfort zone. Access to fresh air, daylight and outside noises, the facility for individual manipulation of room conditions via the control panels and the restrained colours and materials are all part of a rational standard that aims to enhance the occupants' concentration on their daily business rather than divert them from it. And it is the façade element with full storey-height glazing – the most important achievement of this meticulous design process – that fully and utterly exploits the advantage an office tower work place has over one in a low building, elevating the high-altitude desk space to romantic heights; the fascinating view over the city and beyond turns an office chair into a throne.

In the summer of 1993, Helmut Jacoby produced a series of perspective images of the project. At the time, the planning process had only reached design stage; the perspectives, therefore, enabled the architects, in co-operation with Jacoby, to examine important design features and to optimise the images illustrating the projects' desired impact.

These perspective images of the forecourt show the development of illustrations from preliminary sketches to full perspective drawings.

View from the park: The building during the planning stage still with two basements.

To see what architecture is capable of when it is allowed to go beyond standard practice can be seen in the executive floors for the RWE board. The five floors reserved for the company leadership – the top five floors, of course; hierarchy can't be abandoned altogether – are linked by a dramatic internal stairwell landscape that echoes the dynamics of circular movement in its glass-aluminium construction, conjuring up images of steps climbing an alpine landscape. In addition, two sheltered roof gardens in front of the internal, circular boardroom – which is fitted with skylights – and the stone basin in the upper sanitary zone enhance the ambiance of representative elegance; gone is the heavy oak furniture and hunting-lodge décor of the former RWE headquarters.

The architects have shown the old captains of industry of the Ruhr region that good taste is informed by restraint and that elegance evolves around the identification of the essential. Some of the older generation of RWE people may have been taken aback by this sharp contrast to the past, but: modernism remains an obligation even if reform is difficult to swallow.

Paradoxically, the unique capital of the glass tower was informed by the old generation's love for bold statements of power; the disc on stilts located on the rooftop was initially planned as a helipad, a design idea that had far-reaching consequences for the entire planning process. The elevator tower, for example – a fully glazed beauty in its own right, sheathed in a screen of slats and accommodating four panoramic elevators – was attached to the outside of the main cylinder because its top part, extending beyond the rooftop, was not allowed to stand in the direction of the predominant winds. The decision to place the elevator shaft in this way was not reversed when the board decided to scrap the idea of the helipad in 1993 during a phase when economic measures were implemented to improve efficiency, a move that also led to downsizing in the traditional areas of the company.

Christoph Ingenhoven transformed the disc into a symbol, the existence of which was justified by giving it the functions of sun screen and of a base from which the façade-maintenance platform is suspended. A typical crown for a high-rise building that, in combination with the antenna and the elevator tower rising above the rooftop, lends this prototype a suitable label: a sort of halo for the world's first eco-tower.

But is it? Can this building really be ecological? As early as 1995, Frei Otto, Christoph Ingenhoven's mentor in matters of innovation, summarised the dilemma thus: 'The work-place silo that is the office tower is inherently extremely unecological, it is a potential energy waster, it is inhumane. It is easy to save energy in a building like that, and while that is economically sensible it doesn't make it an ecological building by any stretch of the imagination. Ecology requires much more, like the endorsement of all things living.' Christoph Ingenhoven echoes his colleague's evaluation as he considers the fashionable label of an ecological high-rise building: 'I can only say that we attempted to make the building more ecological. For us, this means – and to me that's very important – that we are taking a holistic approach which ranges from meticulously worked-out details, via energy-saving concepts to aesthetics.'

In his brief 1996 essay on the principles of a holistic approach to architecture called 'Evolution, ecology, architecture', Christoph Ingenhoven attempts to identify – with reference to a Far-Eastern-style definition of harmony – the individual aspects of a construction brief with regards to the general impact of the finished product; in this essay Christoph Ingenhoven says: 'Beauty and elegance in architecture are a direct consequence of correct decision-making. Good architecture is often beautiful whereas ugly architecture is rarely good.' And in the chapter titled 'Relaxation' he says: 'The structure, spatial quality or external appearance of buildings must never contradict people's natural requirements or diminish their living environment in any way.'

In what way this rationale has been applied to architecture can be observed in the RWE project. Here, aesthetics are not informed by artistic talent but by a pragmatic stance. It is a pragmatic vision that reveals a sensitivity for complexity and an ability to distil this complexity into simplicity, logic and communication; this is what sets this tower apart from the rest, both in terms of appearance and physical experience. The success of this building is all the more surprising if one considers that this is the first building that Ingenhoven Overdiek und Partner have built. The fact that rational principles have been successfully put into practice within a well-balanced building project, and a debut commission to boot, is down to two factors that have always been vital prerequisites in the creation of reference buildings: an architect capable of analytical thinking and of putting the results of this thought-process into practice, and a client willing to provide the funds and prepared to grant conceptual liberties in order to bring the project to completion. The rare chance to be involved in all aspects and stages of construction, from the design for the building to the selection of furniture – a chance RWE granted their chosen architects Ingenhoven Overdiek und Partner – can, in this case, be justified: we have an openly proud and a proudly open building that is honest, restrained, capable, communicative and – therefore – beautiful. Christoph Ingenhoven, quite uncharacteristically, likes to joke with friends and colleagues by asking them which architect they think has entered the pantheon of architecture with which project; he can, if he's at all worried, sit back and relax: with his first building he has won a seat in the assembly of reason and longevity.

Interview
Christoph Ingenhoven in Conversation with Klaus-Dieter Weiß

You took part in the Frankfurt Commerzbank competition aged only 31, facing formidable international competition and, a complete newcomer, you almost beat Lord Norman Foster to the first prize. What aspects of high-rise construction do you find particularly inspiring?

The design for the Commerzbank building ten years ago inspired us to specialise in and concentrate on projects of this kind. High-rise buildings are so fascinating because it is possible to work on a single project for an extended period of time. A high-rise design brief is a long-term undertaking that demands the highest aesthetic and scientific standards. This includes the façade design and proportions and its connection to the internal structure. In architectural terms, a high-rise building is almost a design object. It involves the process of very detailed designing and re-modelling of a basic form. If the structural components are simple shapes – owing to their dimensions – the details can be emphasised more strongly. As high-rise buildings are by definition expensive to erect, additional efforts and costs in creating an optimised product are always justified. Furthermore, industrial manufacture is today very advanced and therefore ideally suited for high-rise construction. Consequently, the manner of controlling the construction process has also changed considerably. When you have five hundred, eight hundred or a thousand identical elements, as is the case with the RWE façade, you can achieve a hither-to unattainable degree of perfection, using tools such as trial arrangements, simulations, mock-ups and models for which there would be no budget if conditions were different. So, apart from the high-rise building's dominance in urban-planning terms, which sets it apart from horizontally developed urban structures, I welcome the sheer endless amount of possibilities to be explored in a high-rise building project.

Have technical standards changed sufficiently for a new type of high-rise building to emerge?

As the high-rise has again become an issue in the intellectual architectural debate during the last ten years the scope for interesting designs has been expanded. Intellectual accessibility has been created through pressure exerted by developers – in their continued preference for high-rise buildings – as well as by the debate on ecological potentials in building construction. Furthermore, it has probably helped that a number of developers have shifted the focus of the ecological debate on the high-rise building. Technical innovations enable the construction of new types of high-rise buildings, but a huge potential for further development remains. We have new materials at our disposal, such as high-strength concrete, and advances have been made in earthquake safety and the construction of very tall buildings; we can now erect buildings over one thousand metres high – irrespective of whether this is sensible or not. Today, we are dealing with much higher elevator speeds or high-strength and high-performance glass construction that allows a much higher percentage of glazed surfaces in a building. We're discussing natural ventilation, which has, compared to the 1970s, changed the way physical well-being figures in high-rise buildings. We now have new fire-protection measures, enabling the creation of multi-storey zones within a high-rise building for easier internal communication.

The weaknesses of high-rise buildings, particularly those built during the 1970s, are surprising in so far as brilliant historical examples with regards to design and aesthetics have always been available. Frankfurt, with its dense network of skyscrapers, does not provide convincing arguments when it comes to generating enthusiasm for new projects. Berlin is even less inspiring.

Even during its heyday, the skyscraper in America was not always associated with the greatest architects. Developers who embark on large-scale, extremely technical projects may regard the architectural avantgarde with a certain degree of suspicion. Some would say that our style of architecture is somewhat cold, that it displays exaggerated sobriety. But in fact we make every effort to integrate all architectural aspects that people feel strongly about in an attempt to fully endorse the content-based aspects in the brief. Post-modernism has justifiably argued against the modernist doctrine to subordinate form to function. Functionalism was based on a far too limited definition of reality. Building on a human scale must include emotional, physical, psychological and spatial-physiological aspects. In high-rise buildings, questions of style only emerge within the context of the architects' way of working. To be able to carve something of your own identity out of the brief, to add a personal note, a unique, eye-opening quality, now that is worth something, that is architecture.

Is the traditional approach of many developers perhaps informed by the assumption that it is difficult to make a bold architectural statement within the constructional and technical constraints of the tall and narrow space provided by a tower?

Many architects have proved that this is not true. A dedicated architect's prime concern is to reveal a novel aspect in the brief, to inject the brief with a quality that no-one thought a high-rise building could bear. This also applies to the new ecological debate on aspects such as natural ventilation and person-to-person communication. To adopt these qualities in high-rise construction is the central theme in many of the new generation of European high-rise buildings. This is a new quality that is going to have wide-ranging formal, ecological and urban-planning-related effects.

You are engaged in an attempt to discover a new way of building, a new architecture. Is it not one of the principles of architecture to define this notion with form and appearance rather than content and theory?

I think that architects like Mies van der Rohe were fascinated by 20th-century science and technology. But I also think that their fascination was of an artistic nature, that they were not really interested in building a construction along engineering or nature-related aspects. They were probably not even interested in understanding that kind of construction. They were fascinated by smoothness and perfection, by mathematical and constructional potential, by speed and by span. Their fascination was informed by aesthetics, it was concerned with the look of things. We, on the other hand, try to steer away from form as the core content of our approach; instead we prefer to arrive at a definition for form as the result of a process. Architecture is not primarily form, except maybe in superficial public perception. Architecture is, in fact, based on reason and content, of which form is a consequence.

You reproach classic modernism for an artistic impetus contained in its love of simple, geometric objects?

Mies van der Rohe was not universally correct when he coined the formula 'less is more', at least not on a comprehensive level. Bruno Taut made a very valid point: he regarded a canon of colours, a tactile canon of surfaces as absolutely essential for building construction. Mies did not consider this to be important at all. But only these two approaches combined, along with a plethora of other aspects, make architecture complete. An artist may perhaps need to temporarily disengage from his subject in order to achieve something outstanding. But a chair like the one designed by Gerrit Rietveld does not stem from the mind of someone who is interested in improving people's sitting experience. Only if all aspects are endorsed do you arrive at a new way of building. Consequently, we do not need new forms; what is required is the emancipation of contents. We need to recognise the reality-defining elements within theoretical approaches and employ them in combination. Architecture cannot be erotic; architecture creates habitats. In so far, this appropriated projection should never be ideologically hijacked.

There are valid arguments for building a high-rise in the shape of a cylinder. But could it not be argued that, in your approach, you disassociate yourself from form-oriented reception to such an extent that you are no longer able to convey your ideas to a wide audience?

You can't not build a round high-rise simply because it's been done before. On the other hand, there are many sites around the world where we would not opt for a round high-rise. I have less of a problem with the repetition of a principal form than with the perpetual redecoration of a more or less identical form. An architect uses the façade as a carrier, an effective media tool; this way, the architect becomes instantly recognisable and is able to promote him/herself on the market. The question remains, however, if there is any significant content behind this 50-cm deep screen. Consequently, it makes little sense, in my opinion, to revel in the aesthetics of the Rockefeller Center when the core contents of this project cannot be put into practice in a totally novel way. The real innovation was, in fact, to transform the high-rise building into a hybrid and thus make it available to the public, to extend public space onto the vertical plane.

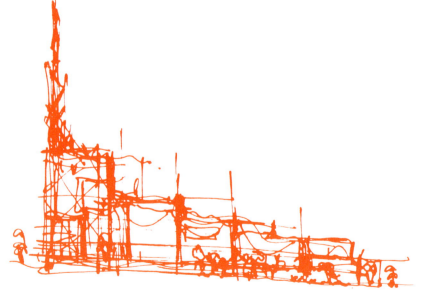

The 1991 competition design already reveals the project's urban-planning concept of 3 high-rise buildings situated behind a line of low-level building blocks with a large park to the rear of the low-level block.

How did the decision to opt for the cylinder come about?
The fact that this building is round can be derived from a number of parameters, such as energy-efficiency. But form must also be derived from the urban context. On top of that, there is the formal aesthetic fascination with that shape. I think that the forms we create are strong and have considerable presence, but they are not overwhelmingly exciting. A high-rise cylinder, 200 m high and with a 40-m diameter, simple, smooth and round like the one we used for the Commerzbank, derives its strength of shape from its stringency and simplicity – not from an over-excited purpose that is purely for effect. The RWE tower is much leaner and on site looks unbelievably slim and dynamic, even if the plans do not convey this very well. On a formal level, we welcomed this result. Architects who build high-rises and say it is not important how high the building will be are not being honest. You cannot develop a shape from contents while strictly adhering to mathematical equations; the design process is not long and detailed enough. A mix of many parameters spin around in the designer's mind; therefore, in order to build an integral object, one parameter must never be allowed to dominate another.

Following post-modernism and deconstructivism with their emphasis on form, do you recognise a trend towards ecological architecture?
There appears to be a flood of ecological high-rise buildings, the Commerzbank and RWE projects having opened the flood gates. Apart form the fact that the architectural resonance only affects the geometry, I would not necessarily consider our style of architecture as ecological architecture. I am much more inclined to say that ecology should today be an integral part of all architectural efforts. I never tire of saying that to think ecologically means, in a way, to think universally. Consider everything that could possibly work. One has to remain open-minded towards all things; after all, people think, act and feel. As far as energy-related details are concerned, the ecological contribution our building makes lies in the fact that we developed a 'negative list' for this building. We were able to design open staircases, an openable façade, but also ceilings with [thermic] storage capacities, a cooling fin element, integrated ceiling elements, control-systems allowing individual control operations, etc. These factors lead to a building that consumes less energy than many other comparable buildings. It makes better use of daylight than other comparable buildings and it has a more effective sun protection system, and with regards to its orientation it facilitates internal office organisation.

Can such a complex set of contents be conveyed in a tangible architectural image?
We want to formally convey our intentions in a very unified and self-contained form that can be taken on board swiftly through a photo, an image or a drawing. This is very important. We live in an age where speed is essential. I can't reverse that trend. All I can do is generate interest for the content through visual images. Form is an instrument of communication.

Essen is not as important a city as Frankfurt, even though it is roughly the same size. Essen's architectural tradition, however, particularly with regards to corporate headquarters designed by luminaries such as Wilhelm Kreis, Alfred Fischer, Egon Eiermann, is quite remarkable. Are you satisfied with the results of your work and the co-operation you have experienced?
Internationally, Essen is completely unknown. But we have been very fortunate in working with the RWE as developer and client. Despite the fact that we encountered many difficult situations the work on this project was very rewarding, as everyone involved gave it their full attention, even the main contractor, who was, in effect, working on behalf of its parent company, the RWE. I was on site almost every day, which was quite easy as our office is not far.

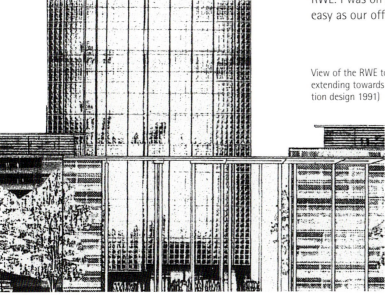

View of the RWE tower with the loggia roof extending towards the Opernplatz (competition design 1991)

Essen central station has two city-centre orientations: the shopping area to the north and the service industry zone to the south. The Passarea project aims to consolidate the station's central position by turning it into the hub connecting the two formerly separated city-centre zones.

Initially, your brief in Essen was predominantly of a town-planning nature. What led to your office designing the RWE-building?

The RWE building competition was indeed of an urban-planning nature. While the central brief was to build two headquarters for Ruhrkohle AG and for RWE, the submitted design nonetheless had to be an urban-planning concept.

What were your urban-planning goals?

We were concerned that we would end up with an unacceptably strong concentration of high-rise buildings and that the two headquarters envisaged in a single competition would unduly compete with each other. In order to avoid this dilemma, we placed the high-rise building for Ruhrkohle AG near the railway station and the RWE building at a rather surprising location next to the Aalto theatre, about 100 metres due south. This allowed us to extend the existing ring of high-rise buildings around the railway station. The choice of location for the RWE building was very convincing because we were able to create a spacious and interesting urban situation in conjunction with the prominent Alvar Aalto opera and the adjacent public park. We then decided to enclose the entire area with a block structure of up to six storeys. By that stage we had covered most of the required development areas in our planning concept.

We then arranged two high-rise buildings, one rectangular block and one circle, behind the block enclosure. The remaining area was made available for a generous public park. The fact that we placed the two high-rise buildings at a certain distance from one another, and that we were the only competitors to provide a large free space within the block surely contributed to our winning the competition – irrespective of the architecture.

To what extent, if at all, was the RWE-building design, which was very much informed by the urban-planning context, modified during the planning process?

During the design process the RWE-building substantially increased in height. Placing it behind the block enclosure had the effect that the loggia roof – which marks and continues the block enclosure in front of the building while at the same time cutting a gap into it – created a very public situation: a gradual sequence of public spaces integrating the project into its urban environment. We were able to achieve a similarly strong link to the garden at the rear of the building with the terrace on the 'garden level', which houses large functional areas such as casino and cafeteria. Here, an inclined glass wall facing the lake and a 100-metre cyclopean wall were two important determinants in our planning concept.

The integration of the RWE building into its environment is, for this type of building, quite extraordinary. It is a high-rise that is open-ended towards the ground, yet it is rooted firmly in its urban context. This phenomenon is easily overlooked, although it was a vital and deciding feature from the outset. Once we had agreed on this concept, we began the detailed design process of the tower itself, which was always going to be round, or polygonal, but subsequently underwent a series of modifications, for example in the externally located elevator towers.

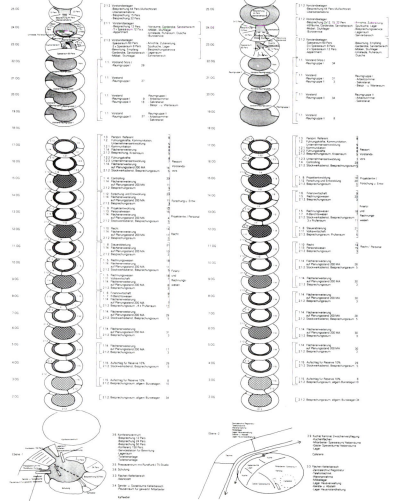

These diagrams show the planned tower's occupancy and functional co-ordination at preliminary planning stage.

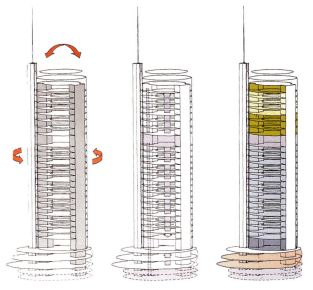

These drawings illustrate the principles of circulation within the flexible office organisation.

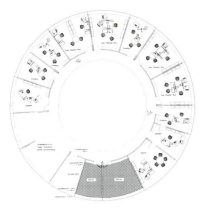
Typical plan – circulation

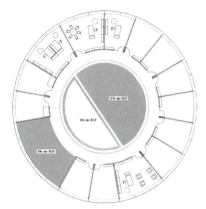
Typical plan – surfaces

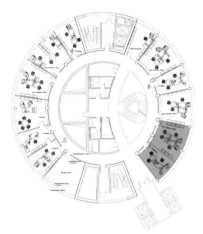
Typical plan – furniture

The plans show possible furniture lay-outs for the trapeziform offices, the relative proportions of core and office surfaces as well as the positioning of the circulation cores. These diagrams illustrate how the functional and technical requirements can be integrated into the compact circular plan.

The characteristic top of the building – which is, quite apart from the building's height, significant for the terminological distinction between skyscraper and high-rise – is also rather unusual. Is it based on an existing example?

The second, external glass layer exceeds the top of the building, articulating an open and transparent termination at the top. There is a building in Düsseldorf which dissolves into the sky, so to speak, and that has fascinated me since I was a child; it is the Wilhelm-Marx-Haus by Wilhelm Kreis, built in 1924. The reinforced concrete skeleton structure with brick cladding ends in a sort of fractured ornament at the top. Behind the double-height roof parapet on top of the roof is a tent-roof covering a water container for fire-fighting. Our design is more functional and does not represent a retro gesture towards Neogothic architecture. The building extends into an open top, with the boardroom and two roof gardens on one level, and a larger terrace on the boardroom roof. All three terraces are enclosed by the glass shell which extends upwards, providing wind protection and allowing their full use despite the considerable altitude.

You have achieved the same degree of transparency at ground level. How did you manage to avoid a solid appearance of the building's core?

A particular aspect of the building's constructional structure is that the transparent and open lobby acts as a link between the public space at the front of the building to the garden at the rear. By placing the building's cores to the sides we created a large free centre space at ground level. We developed a so-called transferral concrete construction, where the forces generated at the centre of the building are transferred to a ring of supports. This construction is visible and comprehensible. It creates a central void in the building's centre that is enclosed by a glass wall on the ground floor. The circular lobby, which remains relatively intimate despite its transparency, is linked to the garden level below, also accessible to the public, via staircases and openings. Both these levels can be used for events as they are independent of the remaining office functions above and do not interfere with the client's safety requirements. Due to the sensitivity of RWE's line of business their security requirements are critical. Nonetheless, in co-operation with the client and their safety advisors we have managed to create a building that is at least visually completely void of barriers and boundaries.

Were you also responsible for the landscape planning?
We appointed Roland Weber, Klaus Klein and Rolf Maas whom we had worked with many times before, as consulting landscape architects; all in all, however we were responsible for landscape planning and we did, indeed, determine the fundamental concept. We prefer to group experts, advisors and contractors internally in order to remain in charge vis-à-vis the client. We build a harmonised team of our choice so that we do not need to consult external partners for areas such as lighting or landscape design; in some cases we might not even be able to appoint external partners anyway. The interaction and dovetailing of internal and external spaces and aspects are so narrowly defined and so crucial to this project that we simply could not imagine outside capacities deciding on, say, the surface for the driveway or designing the water features, without our active input.

To what extent were you able to influence interior design and furniture options?
The brief included all aspects of interior design including the provision of equipment and material options for the entire building.

Right down to the last office chair?
We were sole architects for all special areas; for standard products, such as office furniture, we had an advisory role. We were responsible for the entire interior concept except for two offices for the RWE board.

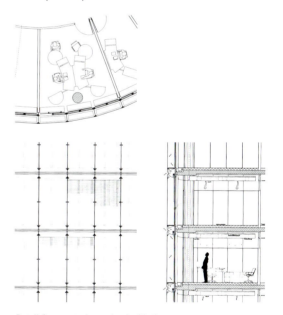

Detail from a study on the double-layer ventilation façade; April 1993.

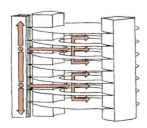
The three-storey-concept, with its internal stairwells, enables unrestricted communication within the office organisation, which typically spans several floors.

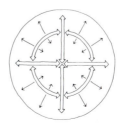
The circular plan and the ring corridor allow for plain and clear orientation.

To what extent were you involved in the invitation to tender, awarding of contracts and costing?
Any architect who leaves these activities to others loses his or her influence over the building. It may be a burden but it is necessary for the building process. It is imperative that the client can trust the architect; these days this trust has, alas, largely evaporated. Clients tend to think that architects will prefer to build expensively because they are paid a percentage of the total building costs. When architect and client get together to work out a sensible budget, the architect should be granted a certain amount of influence over the project. Only when the architect himself is responsible for the invitation to tender, awarding of contracts and costing will he be able to creatively evaluate costs. So-called value engineering is often just a pretty term for a nasty way of doing business. However, interpreted correctly it describes what architects are able to achieve if they are in charge of these matters – an evaluation with the aim of identifying the essential and the unimportant.

You mentioned Bruno Taut and the significance of colours and tactile surfaces. How did you, in this respect, choose materials for the building?
Due to its prominent glass and aluminium surfaces, the building exudes cool perfection. In our selection of materials we made sure that they would be used as authentically as possible, that they did not 'pretend' to be a different material. Following this notion, aluminium extrusions are finished with aluminium paint or are anodised so they maintain their metallic surface; glass is not tinted or mirrored; natural stone has not been polished but retains its naturally rough quality; wood has been varnished so delicately that its pores remain open, it was virtually just oiled, so that the grain, colour and even the scent of the wood is preserved. It was a vital criterion in the selection of materials to leave their inherent qualities untouched. A further criterion was the ability of selected materials to age 'gracefully' and to develop a suitable patina. This may seem a little strange when applied to glass or aluminium, but an anodised aluminium surface does develop a certain patina, it absorbs the colours and the light of its surroundings. Anodised aluminium is able to change its colour quite dramatically, reflecting the different times of day, the seasons and ambient colours; the anodisation and the ability to absorb ambient qualities create a smooth, velvety surface. These qualities help reduce the cool and stringent aspect of the building. This effect is further enhanced by the generous gardens and the building's overall reticence in the material and colour schemes. The building's colour undergoes subtle changes from a greyish white to a whitish grey. All in all there must be around 10 to 12 colours in the scheme, underscored by materials such as aluminium, glass, grey-blue painted steel and the natural stone floor made from grey-green Bergell gneiss. Due to its sandblasted surface, the floor appears very light and rough, very stone-like. Because the subtle shine of the gneiss has been broken it appears mat, absorbing ambient qualities by reflecting the colours and light effects. The ambiance inside the building, behind the cool glass layer, is smooth and soft, accentuated by structured surfaces.

What aspects of the RWE project were significant for your professional and your office's development?
The size and character of the brief, plus the fact that the competition specifically invited architects to design an ecologically-minded high-rise building, a requirement we had never been asked to meet before.

The tips of the Frankfurt, M., Messeturm and the New York Chrysler Building respectively, compared to the transparent top of the RWE tower. Ingenhoven's initial sketch for the competition illustrates his re-interpretation of a building top by giving it a purpose and by allowing the façade structure to fade into the sky thanks to the transparent glass façade that extends beyond the top floor.

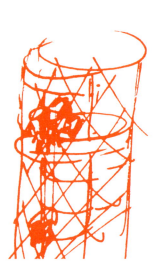
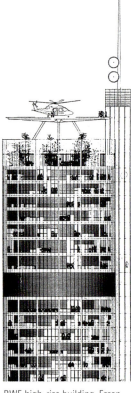

RWE high-rise building, Essen   Messeturm, Frankfurt, M.   Chrysler Building, New York

So the ecological requirements were defined in the brief?
The brief only included key-words in an attempt to partly define ecological aspects. But since we had never dealt with high-rises before, only ever dreamt of working on one...

...you had a dream of working on high-rise projects?
Yes, I presume all architects share this dream.

Would you find it fascinating to work in a high-rise building yourself?
Yes, I find it fascinating, because you feel removed from the outside world and you have this wide, panoramic view. That's why I would find it bizarre to build high-rises with cut-out window openings that restrict the view. Viewed from the inside, the RWE building's façade has a 100% glass content. The internal ceiling height of 3 metres is totally unrestricted by the fully glazed external layer. This increases the influx of natural daylight, permits an almost panoramic view and underlines the building's general aspect of openness, which is inherent in the building's plan. To ruin this effect with banisters, drop ceilings, lintels and wall cladding would be tragic.

Why do you think high-rise buildings are so unpopular, given that most people will only spend their working day there? A few years ago, a critic was still referring to the 'dinosaurs of architecture'.
High-rises had and still have a negative image because they minimise the influence people have on their experience of space – the constant and intense sunlight beaming into the offices aggravates this situation further. Usually high-rises are fitted with automatic air conditioning and automatic sun protection: the individual has no influence over the conditioning of his or her environment. This problem can be solved by building a two-layered façade with a 50-cm cavity in which simple equipment is installed. You can use totally transparent glass and install slatted sun screens for variable dimming of sunlight flooding into the room. These possibilities have only recently appeared in the architectural debate and are used in our building for the first time. The building is naturally ventilated; the individual is able to regulate the climate of the room he/she works in via an individual control panel next to the door or, much easier, by opening the window. Even under extreme conditions the building can be naturally ventilated for around 9 months of the year. There are, of course, climatic support systems, but we have always regarded them as a last resort. On the other hand, since we were dealing with an almost experimental technology, we were prepared to accept the client's safety demands, towards which we were very sympathetic. In future projects we will, of course, endeavour to go even further down the ecological path. You see, even taking the step from full to limited air conditioning you already release funds and surfaces that can be put to use in another way.

What were you able to achieve for your vision of the project in the discussions on fire regulations?
Until you reach high-rise level you are allowed to incorporate a maximum of two floors within a single fire compartment. There are buildings with more than two floors in one fire compartment, where the installation of sprinkler systems resulted in an exemption from building regulations. In our project, we were able to navigate around fire regulations on corridors and corridor walls to a large extent, enabling us to use glass walls in some parts for increased transparency within the building. This is the advantage of high-rise projects: the architect can ensure that the general co-operation with the relevant authorities includes separate discussions on special building permissions for individual parts of the building, incurring a slightly increased workload but at the same time enabling the architect to work around building regulations. Our building was constructed in the spirit of building regulations, but we did not follow them word for word.

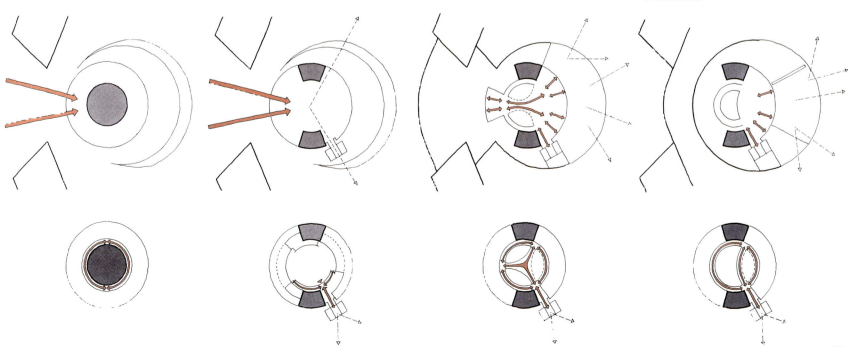

The pros and cons of either a central or two de-centralised cores were examined in diagrammatical drawings. In view of the desired transparency of the lobby and garden-level floor as well as the desired flexibility of the central core in the top floors, the architects opted for two externally positioned cores that house the emergency stairwells, fire brigade elevators and services shafts.

Commerzbank AG, Frankfurt, M., office floor plan (M 1:1000)

You have consulted a number of prominent experts in order to explore and analyse the problematics of high-rise building as comprehensively as possible. What are your experiences?

Not only did we intend to be actively and comprehensively involved in issues such as load-bearing structure planning, technical installations and physics but we were also interested in working out a philosophical approach to building an ecologically sound high-rise building. This led to our office asking Frei Otto to be our mentor, our wise teacher and discussion partner. It was one of the most memorable experiences of my professional life to witness how someone manages to close the generation gap by selflessly giving sound advice. Together we attempted to redefine high-rise building. We set up a list of negative criteria of existing high-rise buildings and we found that an ecological high-rise first of all needs to be more of a 'proper' high-rise building, one that manages to cope with aspects of communication, of vertical and horizontal transparency. Conventional high-rise buildings often have a very poor interior quality. The storeys are usually almost hermetically sealed, making interaction virtually impossible. In spatial terms, regarding the building's boundaries, the room configuration or vertical transparency provided by, say, atriums or open staircases, they have nothing to offer. The only exceptions are spectacular hotel towers, but that kind of building style is not transferable to office buildings.

As far as questions of the plan and technical construction are concerned, are your designs for the Commerzbank in Frankfurt and the RWE building in Essen somehow related?

No, they are completely different. Sure, both have a circular plan, but due to specific functional requirements for areas beyond office planning the Commerzbank tower evolved into a circle with a 45-metre diameter, where it would have made no sense at all to fill the outer part of the circle with offices, as this would have produced a far too large interior surface. The RWE tower, on the other hand, with a diameter of only 32 metres, allowed offices to be arranged in a ring, connected by a circular corridor, making the core available for services and vertical circulation. This concept allowed us to develop a balanced volume-to-surface ratio; it also helped us achieve a very compact building. The building's compactness was further enhanced by placing

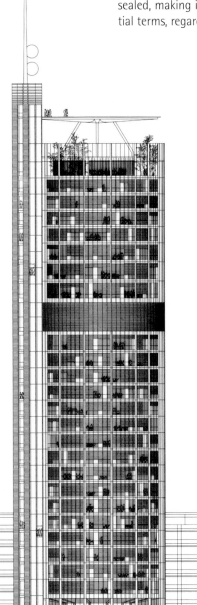

View from the park (M 1:880)

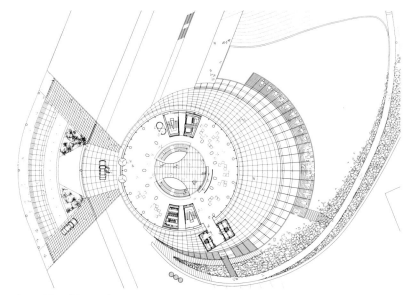

Ground floor (M 1:1000)

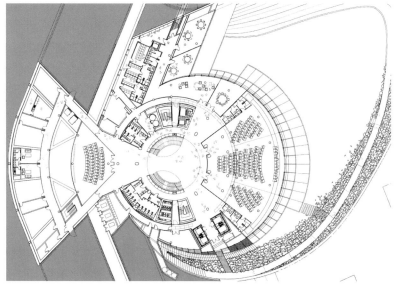

The lobby on level -1 (M 1:1000)

stiffening cores near the external layer. Some floors were thus equipped with internal staircases, a lobby and generally more internal space. We were determined to reap the benefits of this concept even after it was decided to scrap the idea of a rooftop helipad.

How flexible is the organisation of offices with regards to the building's plan?
We employed a completely flexible system of partition wall elements, so that large rooms could be created if required. This kind of flexibility needs to be envisaged, because the hardware, i.e. the building's structure, has an expected life-span of around 80 years, during which a number of fundamental changes in usage is imaginable. We are, nonetheless, more or less dealing with a cell structure of a relatively permanent nature. The single office is going to be around in 20 or 30 years time. Whether large open-plan offices, combined offices or offices designed for specific functions will still exist remains to be seen, but the single office type appears to be a consistent factor for a variety of uses.

Can the cylinder be partitioned and partly let?
This has in part already happened. There are two independent user-units that share facilities and services but in fact represent two different kinds of usage. It was planned to include one or two further RWE-related occupants if this was required, but given the current occupancy this appears rather unlikely.

From my train window I had the impression that, from afar, the glass façade appeared uniform. Why do you think this is?
When you look at the building from a distance the perception of the glass façade is principally that of the entire glass shaft, not the 'excerpt' you see from the pedestrian perspective, where more activity and detail create a different situation. From a distance you don't really see a closed façade in the sense of it being sealed, but there is an impression of...

...a detailed façade structure?
Yes, what we have always referred to as a 'high-rise in aspic'. The observer sees the external aspic layer – that's the external glass layer. The unity of the shape created by the glass façade that appears to be holding everything together was crucial to our vision of the building; it is responsible for the minimalist appearance of the tower, like a line drawing. We did not want to disrupt this smooth external appearance – so full of tension - with sections. As soon as sections are added, like in the Seagram Building, the message becomes classicist. We did, however, contemplate the aerophysical function of sections in order to create the ne-cessary vorticity. But we discovered that the small ope-nings create sufficient vorticity so that sections were not required.

13th floor
(M 1:1000)

18th floor

23rd floor

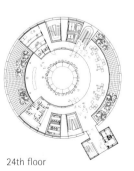

24th floor

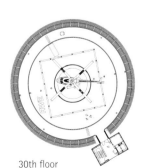

30th floor

View from the Alvar Aalto theatre (M 1:880)

The lobby appears virtually transparent: free from any load-bearing or circulation structures inside the internal core, the view from inside and outside is completely unrestricted.

Main station Essen with RWE high-rise in the background

Façade detail with elevator tower and helipad (M 1:360)

Why is vorticity necessary?

A shark's skin, for example, is not at all smooth. The speed at which it travels through the water is increased through the roughness of its skin because it creates small turbulences in the water which improve the shark's aerodynamics. Aircraft, for example, are painted with a rough paint, thereby reducing fuel consumption substantially. It is quite similar with buildings. The wind blowing against a building should preferably surround the building like a laminate, it should 'hug' the building closely. In the vicinity of the window-ventilation inlet vents we require a certain amount of vorticity so that air can be blown into the vents by winds coming from various directions. For the RWE building we conducted a number of wind trials, like micro and macro series, to ensure the surrounding area does not suffer uncomfortable wind conditions. The driveway and public spaces must not, for example, be exposed to eddy winds. We conducted numerous scientific tests, for example to find out how much wind pressure will be exerted on the façade in various weather conditions, and what effect this has on the air-purging of the space between the two façade layers. We tested the possibility of natural ventilation. We also conducted wind-tunnel tests that delivered the relevant data. We began the sequence of tests and experiments at an early stage so we could develop the façade accordingly. We then worked with experts from the façade manufacturer Gartner, several construction engineers and other façade experts on developing the façade; we made mock-ups, models and executed design studies and technical arrangement trials to test the façade's qualities with regards to air-purging, cleaning and maintenance, pre-fabrication and modularity. This represented a complex and long-winded design process which finally resulted in a one-storey-high pre-fab part. Thousands of these pre-fab parts were manufactured relatively fast for on-site fitting.

Your proposal for the redesign and extension of the railway station, part of the Passarea project, could be described, like the RWE tower, as symbolic. Is this a constant element in your work?

By pulling down the roof to floor level in some parts we have achieved a very high degree of formal stringency which will generate a strong line-drawing effect while keeping the urban profile of the building, quite literally, very low. We tried to strike a balance between the towers and the station's low-level curve. Actually, when you approach the city you first see the station from above; this is an interesting spatial perception creating a real city centre. With this project, Essen has finally acknowledged its urban core.

In the past, the tastefulness and solidity of arts-and-crafts prevailed, and it still triggers nostalgia today – look at Berlin...

I'm afraid that's over. This is a retrospective melancholy that I know and share. But I think we managed to endorse this quality in the RWE building in a different way, by executing control over the industrial manufacturing process where quality can be achieved in the detailing and in repetition.

View from the park (model)

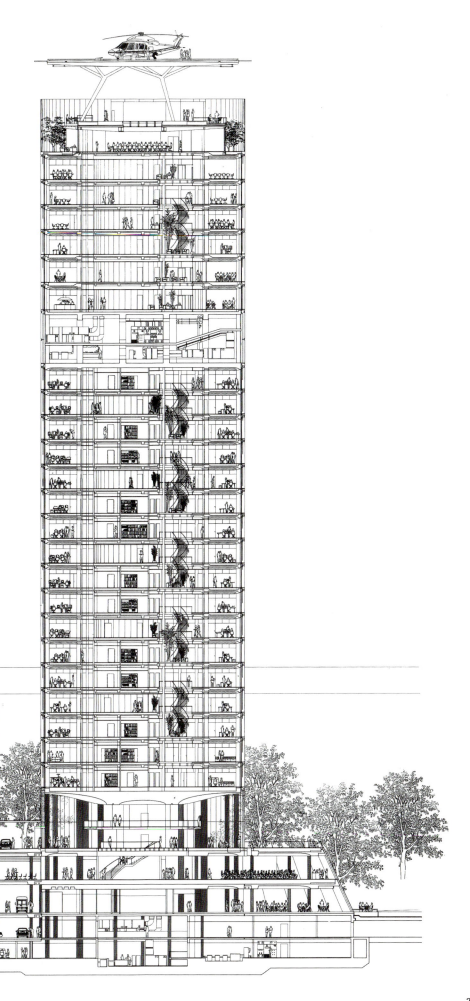

This section (M 1:560) through forecourt and tower shows the adaptation of the basement floors into the building's sectional shape between street level and underground parking level; it also shows the tower's structural composition.

Tour

The public space between the Aalto theatre and the RWE headquarters is dominated by an oversized road interchange (Rolandstr./Gutenbergstr. and Rellinghauser Str.). The re-design of this area is based on a reduction of through-traffic in the wider context of traffic planning for the area covering the 'Stern' service industry zone to Essen central station. By relocating the remaining public transport routes (tram and bus) to the former road junction's periphery it is possible to create a high-quality urban space. Via the Rellinghauser Straße, the new piazza now links Essen's city centre shopping district and the central train station to the north with the Aalto theatre, the city park and the Saalbau to the south. The newly developed urban areas along the Rellinghauser Strasse and Gutenbergstrasse will become more attractive and sought-after thanks to the integration into this urban development scheme. The Aalto theatre, which to date is oriented exclusively towards the city park, also benefits by acquiring an additional attractive orientation.

The municipal park is connected to the RWE park and gardens via the Opernplatz, the forecourt and the driveway as well as the building's peripheral terrace. The interconnection of city centre parks, re-designing surrounding streets and planting new street vegetation as well as the design of new parks and gardens on site formed an integral part of the overall landscape concept.

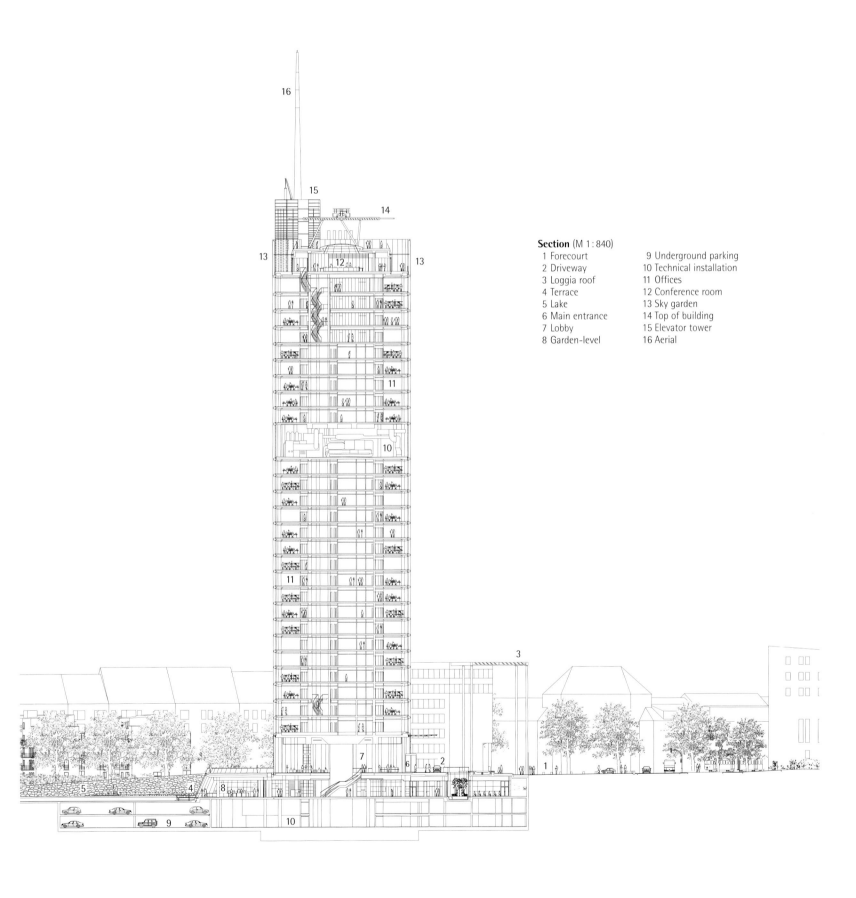

Section (M 1:840)
1 Forecourt
2 Driveway
3 Loggia roof
4 Terrace
5 Lake
6 Main entrance
7 Lobby
8 Garden-level
9 Underground parking
10 Technical installation
11 Offices
12 Conference room
13 Sky garden
14 Top of building
15 Elevator tower
16 Aerial

The building's construction principle as well as the load-distribution characteristics on ground floor level are reflected in the transversal lobby structure and the architectural concrete supports and wall slabs. Ceiling sails with indirect lighting are hung into the approx. 2-m-high reinforced concrete ceiling.

Ground floor (M 1:830)
1 Opernplatz
2 Forecourt
3 Driveway
4 Main entrance
5 Porter
6 Glass elevators
7 Lounge
8 Open space
9 Lobby
10 Elevator lobby
11 Water basin
12 Light well
13 Terrace
14 Lake-site terrace
15 Lake
16 RWE park

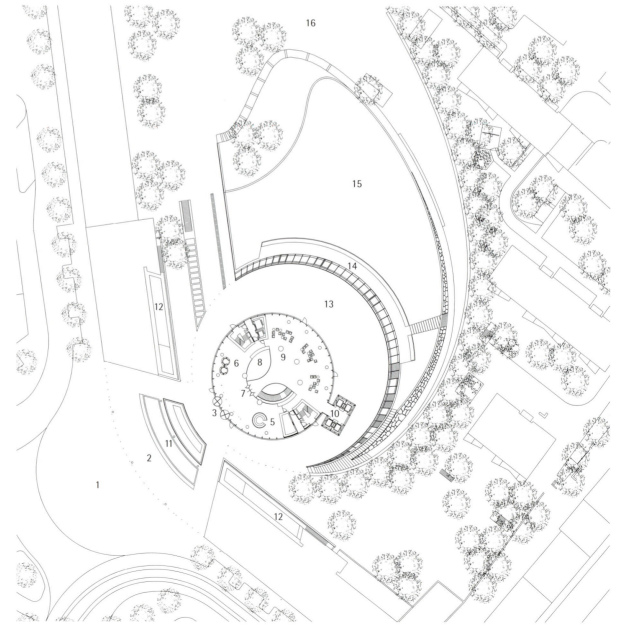

Staff can ascend from the underground parking to the entrance lobby with the two glass elevators. Security checks are conducted in the lobby's glazed turnstiles.

The interior restaurant and conference rooms on the garden-level floor receive daylight through elongated lightwells adorned with water basins and bamboo trees.
Right: the sickle-shaped ceiling cut-outs between ground floor and garden level-floor structurise and extend the lobby. They accommodate a curved interior stair and allow the basement to be lit by daylight.

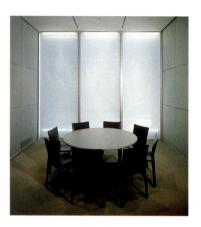

Garden level (M 1:900)
1. Elevator lobby
2. Glass Elevators
3. Connecting stairs
4. Foyer
5. Cafeteria
6. Restaurant
7. Bar
8. Dining rooms
9. Serving point for meal
10. Kitchens
11. Lounge
12. Conference rooms
13. Light well
14. Lake-side terrace
15. Lake
16. RWE park

The garden level links the tower with the RWE parks and gardens. A natural difference in height allows the tower's park-side basement to be lit by daylight. All restaurant and conference rooms are organised in a ring around the tower's circular plan.

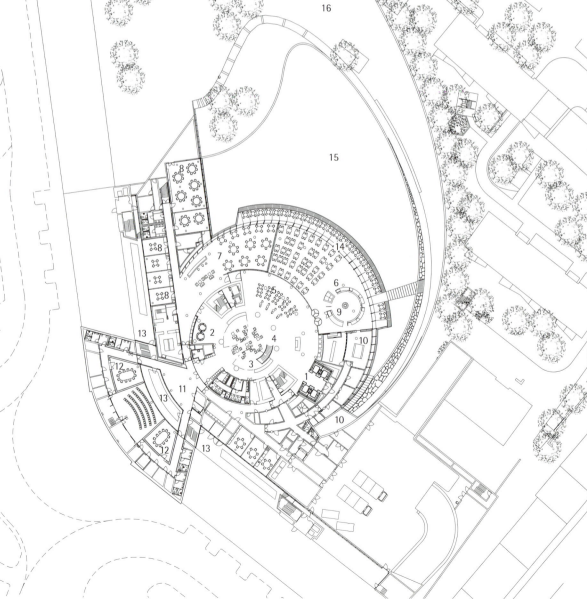

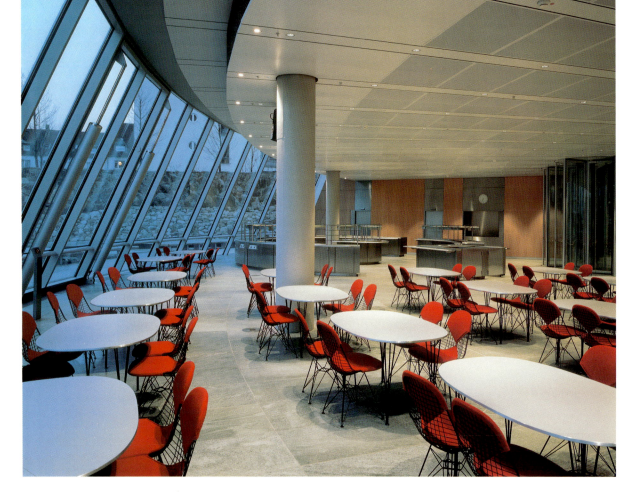

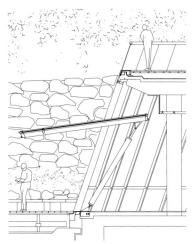

The staff restaurant and dining rooms in the garden level are oriented to the park and the lake via a slanted, floor-high cockpit façade. The terrace situated immediately in front is made accessible by means of hydraulic gates and connects the interior with the outside space.

The lake and the undulating natural stone wall are the main features of the RWE parks and gardens. The lake is fed through a waterfall that springs from between the natural stone wall and the building's foundation. A path for RWE-staff runs alongside the lake and links up with the public footpaths.

Access to all floors is via the free-standing elevator tower. The unrestricted view from the glass elevator cabins and the glazed connecting passages facilitates orientation.

Above: The elevator cabins and control panels were designed in co-operation with Thyssen specifically for this project.
Left: The front-of-elevator lobby on the ground floor is further highlighted by downlights integrated into the stiffening frame of this two-storey zone.

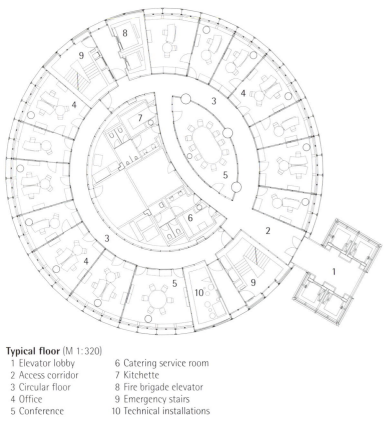

Typical floor (M 1:320)
1 Elevator lobby
2 Access corridor
3 Circular floor
4 Office
5 Conference
6 Catering service room
7 Kitchette
8 Fire brigade elevator
9 Emergency stairs
10 Technical installations

Due to the circular plan of the building, the offices have a larger surface area towards the windows; the auxiliary zone towards the interior has been reduced to the necessary minimum. The interior walls, glazed at the top, accommodate storage units and control panel.

The offices are ventilated and lit naturally via a double-layer glass façade. Various degrees of daylight access can be individually controlled via highly effective sun-protector slats and semi-translucent textile anti-glare screens.

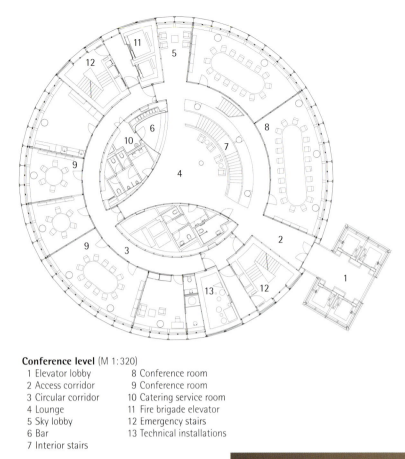

The conference rooms on the conference level are organised around an interior core featuring interior stairs and lounges. All conference rooms can be individually lit and darkened and are equipped with all the necessary devices for presentations and conferences.

Conference level (M 1:320)
1. Elevator lobby
2. Access corridor
3. Circular corridor
4. Lounge
5. Sky lobby
6. Bar
7. Interior stairs
8. Conference room
9. Conference room
10. Catering service room
11. Fire brigade elevator
12. Emergency stairs
13. Technical installations

Ceiling-cut-outs and glazed interior stairs link user zones stretching across several floors. Recreational areas and lounges are located in the interior zones along with the relevant catering service equipment.

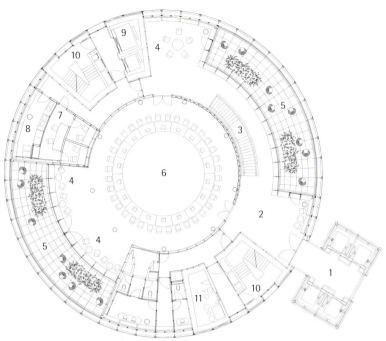

Conference room (M 1:320)
1 Elevator lobby
2 Access lobby
3 Interior stairs
4 Informal meeting area
5 Roof garden
6 Conference room
7 Technical supervision
8 Catering service room
9 Fire brigade elevator
10 Emergency stairs
11 Technical installations

Thanks to a glass dome and storey-height glazed windows the circular conference room and its auxiliary zones such as technical supervision, communication and technical installations benefit from virtually unrestricted daylight. The two semi-circular roof gardens in front of the windows provide superb views over Essen and the entire region beyond.

Roof terrace (M 1:320)
1. Roof terrace
2. Glass dome
3. Elevator machine
4. Emergency stairs
5. Technical installations

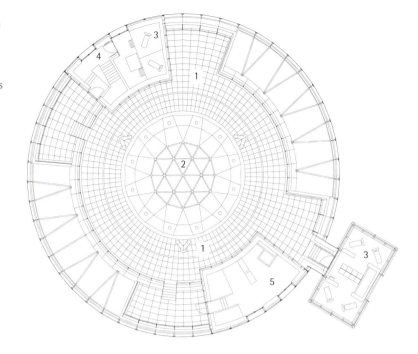

Above the roof terrace, a raised circular steel structure and an extended glass screen form the top of the building.

The slats serve to divert daylight and to screen the conference room below from direct sunlight. Natural daylight and artificial light are both reflected by the aluminium slats' surface.

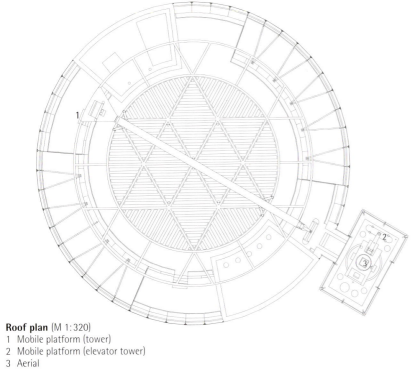

Roof plan (M 1:320)
1 Mobile platform (tower)
2 Mobile platform (elevator tower)
3 Aerial

Top of building (M 1:320)
1 Offices
2 Interior stairs
3 Conference room
4 Informal meeting area
5 Roof terrace
6 Glass dome
7 Mobile platform (tower)
8 Mobile platform (elevator tower)
9 Elevator tower
10 Aerial

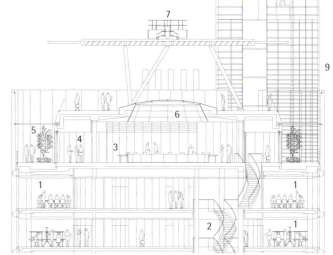

The free-standing elevator tower extends above the office tower; the aerial rises from the top of the elevator tower and forms the tip of the 162-m-building. The elevator tower's construction is based on a fully glazed load-bearing steel structure with external sun screen slats.

Support Structures
Michael Dickson

Many of the experiences we made during our participation in the competition for the Commerzbank Frankfurt headquarters, which ran parallel to the RWE competition, were incorporated into the planning for the new RWE headquarters on the former Stern brewery site in Essen.

In Frankfurt, the 200 metre-high tower with an external, cylindrical glass façade was erected above a low-level, mixed-use building complex with direct access to the two existing Commerzbank buildings and the underground station. The tower is, effectively, a tube with peripheral stiffening and a smooth cylindrical exterior that offers minimum wind resistance. From the double-height entrance upwards, the tower is divided into five sections comprising 8 floors each, with open-plan engine rooms situated between each section. The four voids between the square office plan and the glass cylinder are known as lenticular 'air gardens'. All offices benefit from an individual micro-environment with a high degree of 'outside awareness' and low running costs, generated by the thermal mass of the reinforced concrete composite construction, the vacuum air extraction and the light-weight-construction floor; every office has a view of the internal atrium and the city below.

Our successful participation in the RWE competition allowed us to develop, in co-operation with König & Heunisch and HL-Technik of Munich, the ideas generated during our work on the Commerzbank project. At 32 metres, the 30-floor RWE tower has a slightly smaller diameter than the Commerzbank tower, rendering the inclusions of openings in the ceilings for daylight access and ventilation superfluous. We also applied a completely different stability strategy to the RWE tower which is based on concrete ring cores. But the RWE tower has inherited a number of features from its 'predecessor', such as the double-glass façade; the smooth, cast intrados forming a thermal mass in conjunction with the ventilated girders for cooling purposes, and the division of the building into 'villages' each comprising three floors and each housing a department of the complex corporate structure of RWE AG.

The shell, which is based on a construction outlined below, was erected by Hochtief. In the following chapter, we will take a closer look at the preliminary design for the load-bearing structure and for the services elements. The construction was, of course, modified by Hochtief as building progressed, but the finished building nonetheless retains many of the crucial principles of the preliminary design.

Model of Commerzbank AG, Frankfurt, M.

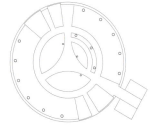

Above: This diagram illustrates the circular plan's congruity of the construction concept, the circulation system and surface economy.
Right: The logic behind the tower's load-bearing structure can be seen very clearly in this night-time photgraph. Thanks to the glass façade, this structure is visible and thus forms part of the aesthetic concept.

The tower

The peripherally located offices have fully glazed floor-to-ceiling exterior walls. The occupants are able to regulate the offices climate by opening the windows towards the 50 cm wide glazed buffer zone provided by the façade with its two glass screens. The office ceilings feature exposed structured reinforced concrete intrados, forming a visually stimulating surface. As the floor base has been designed to accommodate the cooling girders, referred to as 'surfboards', it provides an additional thermal mass. In structural terms, the floor base is a repeated, radially finned plate with a 5.2 metre span resting on the inner and outer column ring. 625 mm thick, it accommodates the ceiling elements and minimises the required volume of reinforced concrete. The internal service zone comprises the core elements, arranged in a beam/plate structure, with drop ceilings. It is separated from the peripheral zone by a 800 mm-ring girder which has gaps to accommodate services devices.

Two cores at the tower's periphery house the emergency stairwells, elevators and risers for the services. These cores measure about 10 x 6 metres horizontally, and the core's wall thickness decreases from 500 mm at the bottom to 300 mm at the top. The circular columns on the building's periphery are made of quality grade 40 architectural concrete and have a decreasing diameter of 600 mm at the bottom tapering to 400 mm at the top of the building, while the dimensions of the internal row of rhomboid columns taper from 950 mm x 450 mm at the bottom to 550 mm x 450 mm at the top. The internal columns stretch from the 2nd to the 17th floor and again from the 19th to the 26th floor. They transfer the load to the cores and main columns, thus ensuring the cores' lateral stability at foundation level.

The foundation of the tower rests partly on chalk stone and partly on sandstone, with the presence of carbon bands between the two layers. The slab foundation is generally 2 metres thick, but around the cores and columns the thickness was increased to 3 metres for extra strength. The different sinking properties of the hard and softer chalk stones were analysed by an earth construction laboratory and the results taken into consideration in the calculations for the lateral dispersal of loads and for additional loads.

To increase flexibility, the floor plates were designed for an applied load of 5 kN/m^2, which includes the light-weight partition walls. In the calculations for the vertical structure, the typical office load index according to DIN 1055 of 2,75 kN/m^2 plus partition walls was applied, with a reduction of up to 40% for live loads.

On the second floor, above the double-height entrance area, a radially deep-finned girder plate – with a height of 2 metres at centre-span tapering off towards the front – clearly defines the lobby. On the 18th floor, where a double-height room without columns was required to accommodate the technical installations, the loads are transferred from the inner zone to the main columns and cores via a system of concrete frameworks, and walls acting as deep girders.

Below: At an early stage, several reinforced concrete structures of different shapes and of minimum weight – for maximum span – were designed and investigated. The vaults in the ceilings maximise the absorbent surface and leave room for the installation of technical components (surfboard).

Stiffening structure

The wind loads were investigated in wind tunnel tests conducted by IFI in Aachen. The tests revealed windloads that far exceeded those to be expected according to DIN 1055, particularly due to the glazed external elevator shaft. An analysis was also needed for the consideration of possible vertical deflection, load eccentricity as well as other deviations and settlements. In linear elastic computer model examinations using models of the building's sub-divisions, simplified equivalent elements were produced that were used in a model of the entire building for examining the tower's transverse stiffening structure. The cores bear the main transverse loads. Although the cores are perfectly capable of absorbing bending stresses around their strong axis without excessive deflection, they are nonetheless integrated on the 18th and 20th floors by a framework structure into a gigantic portal frame. When the planning documents were handed over to Hochtief, the tower's lateral rigidity was examined in a comparison between a rectangular main transverse framework and a more open vierendeel framework. The inner ring of lenticular columns is also integrated into this structure, so that they can further contribute to the tower's flexural rigidity.

The final structural lateral deflection was set at 270 mm, which is the equivalent of a peak value of 500 mm under maximum storm load. The external elevator shafts also add a certain degree of torsion. Acceleration rates were investigated manually, revealing that they were sufficiently lower than the generally accepted limit of 20 mg; their rate of repetitions is 10 years.

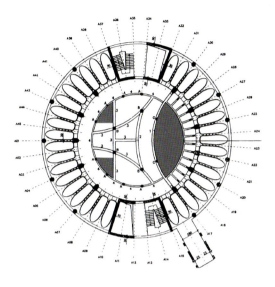

Urban-planning volume model for the macro wind tunnel test.

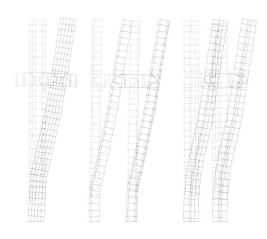

These diagrams show the distortions for load-bearing structures with different degrees of stiffness and for the top load bearing structure in the technical installations floor.

Construction
Lothar Stempniewksi and Heinrich Hacke

A formidable office building
Sub-soil and foundation measures
The site, located in the city centre, is framed by Rellinghauser, Gutenberg, Wiesen and Gärtner Straße on the grounds of the former Stern brewery. Following the demolition of the brewery, an area of around 17,000 m² in site sector south/1 was lowered by c. 13 metres.

A 1 to 2-metre layer of clay-like, marled fine and medium sands (Essen green sand) as well as c. 5 metres of loess and pasture deposits were encountered above the compact yet deeply fissured upper carbon layer of grey sandstone and coal seams.

Along Rellinghauser, Gutenberg and Gärtner Straße the 13-metre deep excavated site was secured with two- and three-fold tied-back timber lining, interspersed with shotcrete. Along the existing buildings on Wiesen Straße a lining of multiple-tied-back bored pile walls with injected concrete filling was built. The poles, 0.7 metres in diameter, were made from concrete strength grade 25. Two residential buildings adjoining the excavated site were braced by a tied-back bored pile wall – pole diameter 0.7 metres – also made from grade-25 concrete.

Due to the deeply fissured carbon rock and the lower ground water level caused by coal mining, a clean water table can be found only in considerable depths.

Construction of individual buildings
Peripheral buildings
The two peripheral buildings are virtually identical in construction terms. They each comprise two levels below ground, a ground level and seven levels above ground. They stand on a combined beam/slab foundation. The structural construction comprises a skeleton structure with load-bearing walls and supports. In order to obtain maximum flexibility for the technical installations, the standard ceilings were designed as 2.5-metre thick flat ceilings. The standard grid span is 6.75 x 7.5 metres. The building's stiffening measures comprised inclined walls and cores. The live load was set at 5 kN/m² on all floors, except in the technical installations zones, where it was set at 10 kN/m².

The tower
By minimising all sections, the concept of a highly transparent high-rise structure as devised by the architect, Christoph Ingenhoven, was successfully turned into practice. The building's outer limits were defined entirely by its horizontal shape.

The three underground levels were all fitted with standard flat ceilings, (30 - 40 cm thickness) with varying span, ranging from the standard 5 metres up to 15 metres for special applications. Large-span ceilings naturally required the inclusion of a set of brows. Due to complex geometrical conditions in the area around waterfall and pond, elaborate shuttering procedures had to be implemented.

The lobby is covered by a spoke-like, 2-metre thick ceiling. At ground floor level, horizontal loads are dispersed via the social/public/corporate-function areas. Since the interior walls in the typical floors must terminate above the ground floor ceiling, the stiffening forces exerted onto the ground floor ceiling need to be transferred to the stairwell cores.

Typical floors
The reinforced concrete works on the typical floors was divided into three stages. For this purpose, a construction joint was incorporated into the circular ceiling plan c. 1 metre parallel to the symmetrical axis. This way, vertical and horizontal works could be carried out simultaneously in alternate week shifts. In general, large-surface-shuttering was employed. In the stairwell cores and the services shafts double external shuttering was used. The corresponding inner shuttering could be used in both concreting stages. The construction of the elevator access areas, comprising two wall panels and the extended corridor ceiling, represents the third concreting stage. Due to the cantilevered construction the third stage followed the second stage at a distance of two storeys. The shuttering for the ceiling was made of prefab ceiling shuttering panels, partly with integrated beam shuttering, which was rapidly continued to the next floor up with a duckbill loader. This way, the three stages were completed before the scheduled two-week period was over.

Typical floor (M 1:283)

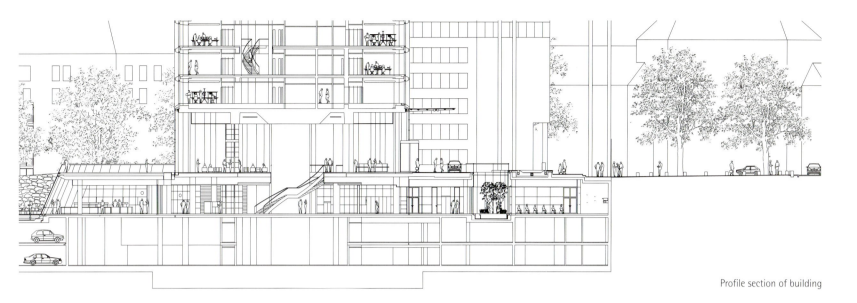

Profile section of building

The ceilings in the typical floors are 25-cm thick flat ceilings. Crucial factors in the ceiling's dimensioning were the minimisation of its own weight and their distortion properties. The incidental load was set at 5 kN/m² in the typical floors and 10 kN/m² in the archive and central zones. The technical installations floor was designed to bear loads of 10 kN/m².

The technical installations floors (17th and 18th) are 7.8 metres high and have joist ceilings with main and side girders. Due to the intense use (public/corporate functions; mixed-use requirements) envisaged for the four top floors, they are fitted with flat ceilings incorporating brows – partly with a high number of ceiling offsets.

The external elevator shaft, 127 metres high, was constructed in accordance with the rest of the building in concrete poured on-site. Its walls are 38 cm, and the ceilings 20 cm thick.

Reinforced concrete works
Foundation slab
Due to the deep fissures in the carbon and the layering of the coal seams (below 60i), the tower was founded on a monolithic foundation slab. 3 - 3.25 metres thick and with a diameter of 36.70 metres, it provides improved settlement characteristics over single or strip foundations. The upper reinforcement was installed in up to ten layers. For the construction of the foundation a steel tube frame with a distance of 1.2 - 1.5 metres between struts was deployed.

During the five-week period of reinforced concrete works on the foundation, a total of 480 tonnes of steel rods were installed. Several cavities for drain pipes, elevator sub-shafts, floor level inlets, ventilation ducts and anchor bolts for the steel supports had to be incorporated. The c. 3,400 m³ of concrete were poured in one day in order to acquire a monolithic foundation. An average hourly rate of 210 m³ was achieved by establishing a combined delivery system using three concrete transport specialists, and by placing four concrete pumps around the foundation site.

To ensure the compression of the concrete in accordance with building regulations, openings were incorporated in the upper reinforcement level. In order to achieve an expansion rate of 55 to 60 cm (table) a fluidity additive was poured into the concrete through the concrete pumps. Due to the extremely high density of the reinforcement, a concrete with an 8 mm corn grading was included in the top and bottom 20 cm of the foundation plate.

Underground levels
The curvature walls in the underground levels were built with large-surface-shuttering, and the supports with steel shuttering. For the vertical parts which would remain visible on level -1 and on ground level, special demands in type of shuttering, gap configuration and quality of concrete surfaces were made. The surfaces were to be smooth and void of any structure; the concrete was to be produced with minimal colour variation and with no pores. The position of element and shuttering panel joints and of the anchor points on the up to 8-metre-high walls were determined by the architect on the basis of the shuttering system. The anchor points were visually highlighted by the addition of anchor cones. A non-suction shuttering type was employed. Due to the varying ceiling thicknesses (30 - 50 cm) and the complex geometry, the ceilings were poured on each individual floor.

The removal of the shuttering from the lobby walls and ceilings instantly revealed the elegance of this huge, partly double-height space.

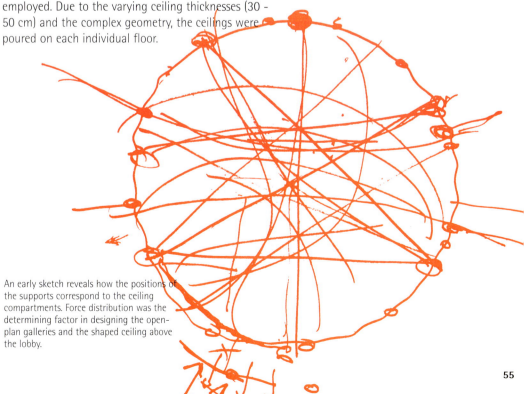

An early sketch reveals how the positions of the supports correspond to the ceiling compartments. Force distribution was the determining factor in designing the open-plan galleries and the shaped ceiling above the lobby.

Ground floor ceiling

The ground floor ceiling acts as a 'load distributor' and is based on an interesting geometry: it consists of an external 50-cm-flat-ceiling ring and a deeply vaulted, 2-m-thick round beam construction in the centre. Shaping this kind of ceiling required the use of three-dimensional shuttering 'pods' made of fibreglass elements. The pre-fabricated, shaped shuttering shells were fastened to a continuous shuttering base and the gaps were lined with 4 mm fibreglass panels, filled and then sanded. Only this way was it possible to produce a ceiling with a seamless visible surface. In order to withstand the pressure of the wet concrete, the entire ceiling construction had to be supported right down to foundation level.

Technical installations floor

The technical installations are located on the 17th floor, which is 7.8 m high. While the stairwell cores were erected conventionally, the remaining vertical building parts were erected in one stage. Due to the extreme density of the technical equipment the five supports inside the interior ring had to be deleted on this floor. This resulted in a beam construction of 1.25 m thickness. It was built with pre-fab shuttering cases fixed to a continuous shuttering base. The outer ring was shuttered with the ceiling elements of the typical floors.

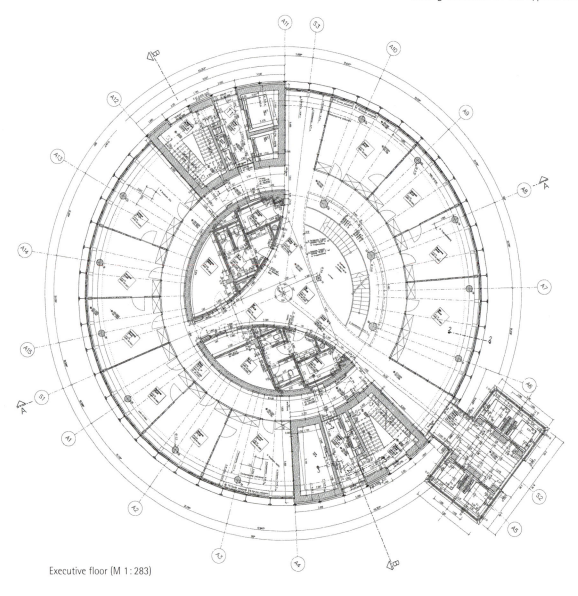

Executive floor (M 1 : 283)

Conference room (M 1 : 283)

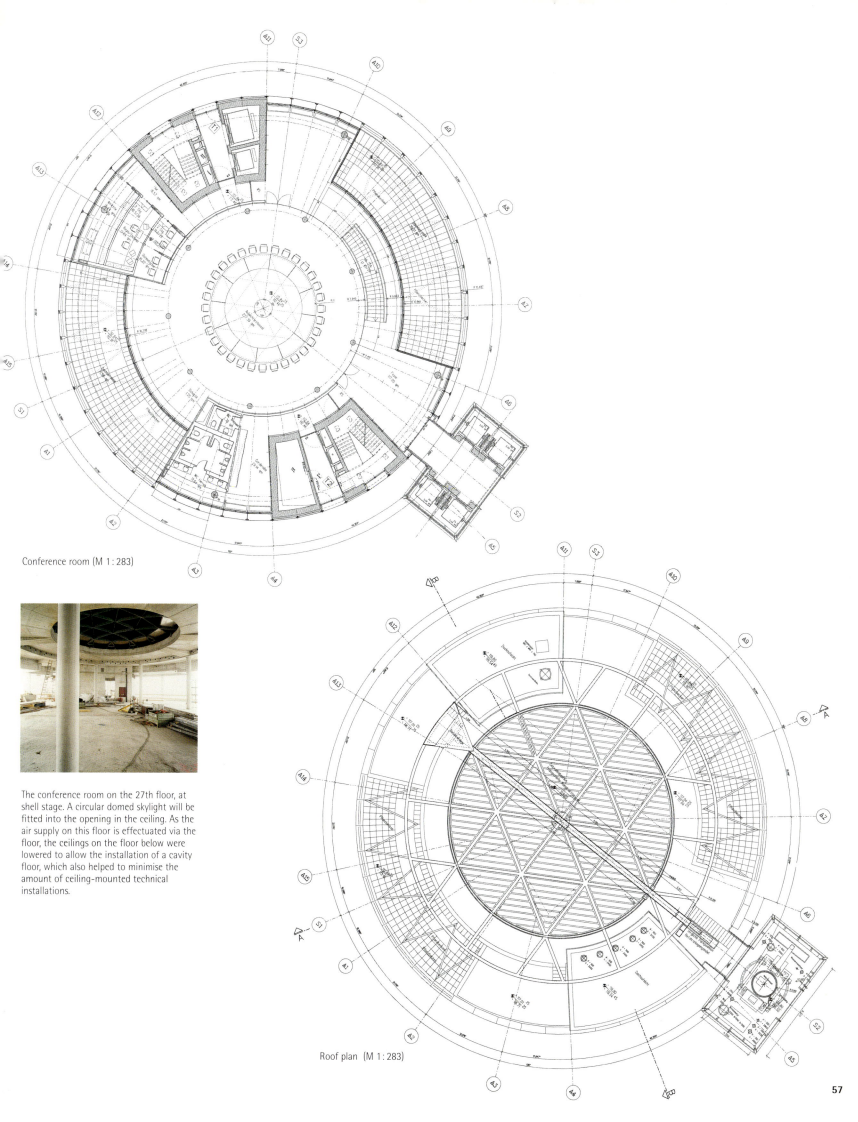

The conference room on the 27th floor, at shell stage. A circular domed skylight will be fitted into the opening in the ceiling. As the air supply on this floor is effectuated via the floor, the ceilings on the floor below were lowered to allow the installation of a cavity floor, which also helped to minimise the amount of ceiling-mounted technical installations.

Roof plan (M 1 : 283)

Concrete composition

A few important factors had to be taken into consideration in the composition of the concrete used for the foundation slab. For example, due to the foundation slab thickness of 3 metres, concrete technology based on bulk concrete had to be applied. Here, concrete compositions were required that prevented excessive warming of the concrete caused by the hydration of the cement, in order to prevent the creation of fissures due to restricted temperature deformations. Following recommendations of the in-house quality-inspectors a blast furnace-cement (CEM III/B 32.5-NW/HS) was used. In order to improve the workability of the concrete, a fluidity (workability) additive was used in addition to the concrete liquefier, which proved very advantageous especially in areas with a high density of reinforcement.

Structural preconditions dictated that the vertical building parts from level -3 to +5 had to be constructed with concrete of a strength grade of 45. In order to keep shuttering periods to a minimum during the winter months, the concrete was switched from a blast-furnace-cement (CEM III/A 42.5) to a Portland cement (CEM I/-42,5 R), as this type sets faster. Generally, the concrete used contained coal tar fly ash and concrete liquefier. For the architectural concrete surfaces on level -1 and 0 an identical colouring was required; therefore, the type of cement had to be selected with the utmost care.

Site logistics
Shell

The delivery of construction material for the tower was routed via two entries to the already completed underground levels, between the peripheral buildings adjacent to Gutenberg Straße and Rellinghauser Straße. Material and staff transport (with a special people carrier) was accomplished with cranes capable of hoisting 2 m^3 concrete containers. Due to the cramped conditions in the ceiling plan and the interior fit-out being carried out eight floors behind concrete-pouring work, the deployment of a concrete-distribution-master with pump was not possible.

The delivery of materials for the underground parking and the residential parts was effectuated via a ramp entry on Rellinghauser Straße. The underground parking, constructed in nine zones, was built right up to the boundary of the northern site zone.

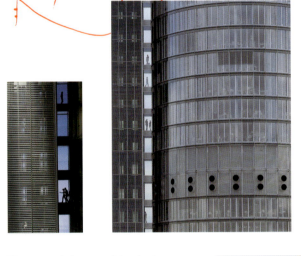

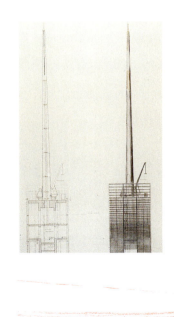

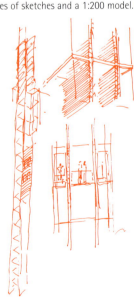

The structural character of the elevator tower and its pin as well as the connection to the main office tower were investigated in a series of sketches and a 1:200 model.

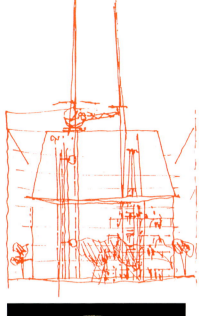

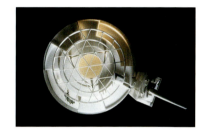

Façade

The polygonal façade (32 m diameter) is made up of 2-metre wide, full-storey-height, two-shell, fully glazed, factory-made façade elements. An element comprises an inner sliding window pane, an outer façade window pane and one half of the so-called fish mouth-shaped, double-sided panel connecting the inner and outer façade shells.

The 120-metre high façade was erected in four stages. For every construction stage, the next floor up was turned into the 'installation floor' for the storey under construction below. A telescopic work platform was installed on each 'installation floor'. The façade elements, bundled into units of three elements for delivery, were hoisted with a rotary tower crane and pulled into the building with a special forklift. A monorail with a crane trolley was installed around the circumference of the building above each 'installation floor'.

A forklift carried a façade element to the edge of the floor and then flipped it into the vertical position; from there, the monorail carried it to the point of installation. The elements of the top three floors had to be installed conventionally by crane.

The 127-metre high façade of the elevator tower consists of a glazed steel frame construction with external aluminium sun screens. The façade elements – 3.6 m high, 2.4 m deep and 7 m wide – were to be installed parallel to the construction of the shell. The 3-tonnes-elements were hoisted with the crane, which meant that the climbing scaffold of the twin elevator access wall panels, which cantilevered from the building plan, had to be coped, which in turn required the erection of a special frame construction. The elevator tower was completed c. six weeks after the installation of the main façade was completed.

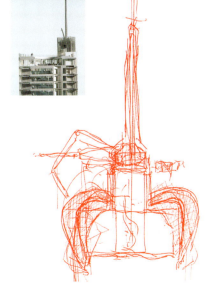

Early models illustrate how the top of the building is made up of several elements. Employing an element-based construction allowed large parts of the steel construction to be pre-fabricated and to be easily mounted by crane.

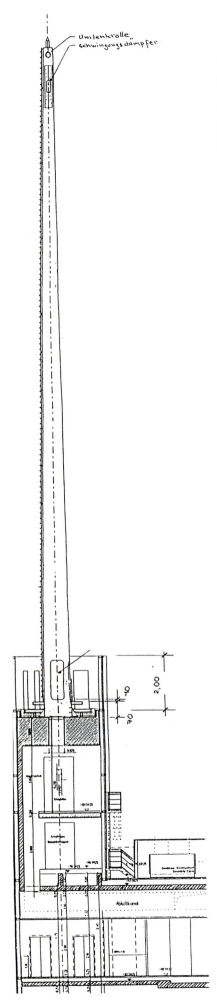

During the course of 1995 Harald Benini, an experienced planning expert at Hochtief, worked closely with the architects to ensure swift communication between architects and site office during the phase when planning and construction were running simultaneously. Numerous detailed sketches were used to examine the complexities involved in sealing the shell to enable the fit-out to begin. The drawings made by Harald Benini were employed to illustrate the complex planning/execution schedule and formed the basis for discussions with the relevant companies.

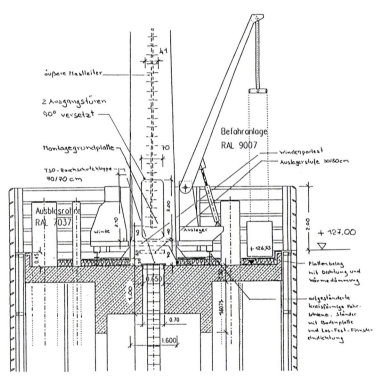

This section through the base of the aerial (1:115) shows how the interior of the aerial can be accessed; the access concept necessitated a fire escape route into the technical control unit below.

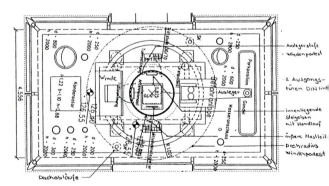

This plan view of the elevator tower (1:130) shows all structural and technical aspects previously co-ordinated by the relevant experts.

Detailed drawings of the aerial on top of the elevator tower (1:200). Shown here: the aerial, shell and technical exit points and the mobile maintenance platform.

The fastened, fully glazed bannister is a standard detail of the RWE project. Its application was tested for several types of installation, for example the roof garden (detail above) or the atria (detail left).

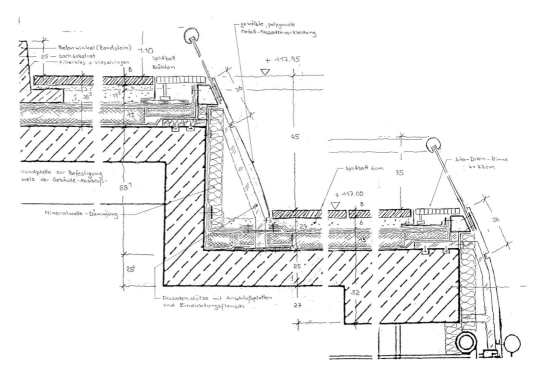

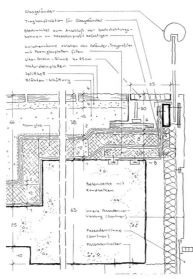

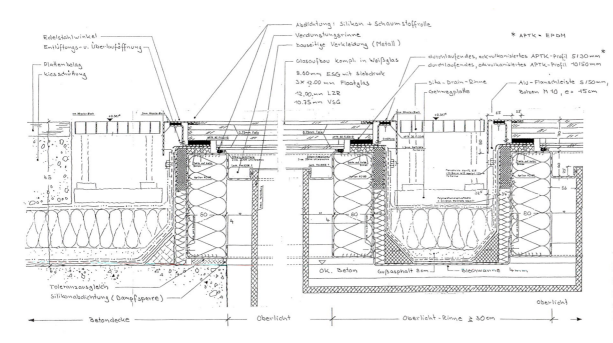

The all-clear to make the detail for the horizontal walk-on glazing inside the façade corridor just above the staff and visitors' restaurants was only given after elaborate optimisations and physical calculations by Hochtief's internal quality management.

Façades

Ulrich Behr
Fritz Gartner
Winfried Heussler

When we, Gartner façade specialists, were invited to work on the RWE project in an advisory capacity, the situation was as follows: after long deliberations the client, RWE, had decided to commission the architects Ingenhoven Overdiek und Partner to build a highly transparent tower. In order to achieve this task in exemplary form, the architects were given the opportunity to develop visionary technologies right up to application stage. During the initial planning stages, a team of structural engineers, technicians, construction physicists and other specialist engineers had composed a problem/solution table, particularly regarding the façade. But the proposed solutions proved largely futile as they were based on preconditions that the other disciplines involved in the project could not accept unreservedly.

On the strength of our experience with different types of façade and results, we had gathered from tests in related fields, we felt that we were able to propose a comprehensive development concept. In close consultation with all parties involved the ideas for solutions generated so far were examined for their readiness to be put into practice. These efforts bore fruit in the form of a façade proposal that met the stringent requirements for internal climate, lighting and the future occupants' contentment. We then formulated a reliable cost-ceiling for this level of development.

In the meantime, the RWE subsidiary Hochtief had taken over the twin roles of main contractor and client/lessor. We were finally awarded the commission to design a façade concept in two stages on the basis of preliminary work and the cost estimate we had produced.

Stage One comprised the entire planning process, including all details ready for execution, fittings, laboratory tests, etc.

Stage Two (several months later) comprised the delivery and installation of all parts along with a comprehensive guarantee for a 'fully operational façade'.

This close-up illustrates clearly that the circular contours of the building are in fact made of 51 straight glass panes: a polygone in disguise.

Above: the diagram shows the recorded hourly air exchange rates inside the offices (maximum rates) in the case of individual office ventilation and in relation to ambient air speeds (in front of façade).

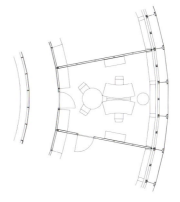

Office on a typical floor (detail)

Description of the façade

The notion of creating as transparent a building as possible is predominantly generated by the client's/occupant's natural desire for optimum use of daylight. As a high daylight quotient is a crucial factor in the quality of a working environment, the glazing should be as clear as possible. The occupants' desire for natural ventilation is also an important consideration for their well-being. The client therefore requested something unprecedented in high-rise construction: that windows can be opened. Finally, to protect the occupants from undue exposure to sunlight a suitable sun screen system was required that would not share the usual disadvantages of interior-mounted sun protection devices.

All of these demands could be put into practice virtually without compromise by applying the concept of a double-glass layer façade with a 50-cm wide space between the two glass walls referred to as a 'façade corridor'. In our case, the exterior wall is made of flint glass that is fastened in only eight places; it is therefore practically invisible from inside and yet fulfils crucial functions: regulating air flow throughout the building and protecting the sun-screens against weather-induced wear.

The inner windows extend from floor to ceiling. Designed as sliding windows they are very user-friendly. To ensure a tight seal when closed, the windows close flush with the glass surface and are pressed into the rebate by a surround-lock. By turning a wheel the window can be opened to a varying degree.

The glass is fitted with a highly translucent insulation laminate. The k-value of 1.2 W/m²K provides good heat insulation in winter and, in combination with slatted blinds, effective sun protection in summer.

Sunshading

External glass envelope

Supporting and ventilation structure

Antiglare device

Internal thermopane glazing

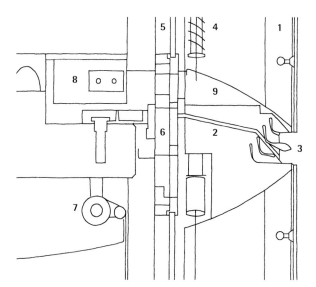
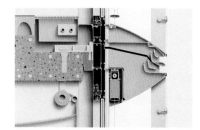

Façade detail
1 Façade construction
2 Façade segmentation
3 Supply and extracted air vents
4 Sun protection blinds
5 Sliding window
6 Thermal separation
7 Anti-glare device
8 Convector
9 Walking platform

Daylight can be diverted and dimmed thanks to the sun protector blinds inside the double-layer façade and the interior anti-glare screen.

In the façade corridor, metal panels in the shape of a fish mouth form the transition from inner to outer glass wall. The minimised ceiling thickness is reduced further to the minimum required air section necessary for adequate ventilation: the outer wall therefore appears largely dematerialised.

The walking platform for the window cleaners in the façade corridor, initially envisaged as a walk-on glass surface, was transferred to the inside of the fish mouth, accessible by raising the top surface of the metal panels.

The design of the air inlet and outlet vents was improved. It emerged that with the appropriate vent design (using slats that facilitate air flow) and without the need for electric flaps, a largely rain-tight section (even in the event of a storm!) was achievable. As only one of these openings was permissible per floor, located at ceiling level, it was necessary that extracted and supply air had to pass the outer glass layer at that point.

An arrangement of in- and outlet vents on top of each other proved unacceptable because extracted air would take the shortest route up to the next floor and enter it in the place of supply air; furthermore, air temperature in the façade corridor and air quality generally would deteriorate with each floor. Incidentally, all concepts that envisage air circulation inside the façade corridor directed from the very bottom to the top of the façade have the same effect. This effect would be acceptable up to a height of only three or four floors.

The simple solution to this problem lies in creating diagonal air streams in the façade corridor, which would require the supply and extracted air sections to be arranged laterally, i.e. next to each other. This can be achieved by alternately perforating the under and upper sides of the double-panelled platforms connecting the inner and outer glass walls. An effective section is achieved with 120 mm wide vents.

The limited outer supply air vents and the perforation of the platform panels act as a wind-breaker to oncoming wind, thus preventing disruptive draught when windows are opened, even at considerable heights.

The slatted blinds in the façade corridor have virtually the same effect as exterior sun protectors. The energy of the sun's rays beaming down on the building is absorbed by the slats; this causes the slats to heat up, but the secondary heat transmitted by the slats remains within the infrared range and is largely deflected from the interior by the insulation glass. Adjusted appropriately, the blinds deflect more than 90% of solar energy from the building's interior. The exterior glass wall protects the blinds from wind, humidity and other climatic elements, so that even fitted to a high-rise building their safe and virtually maintenance-free operation is ensured over many years.

The façade is cleaned from a maintenance platform suspended from a roof-top bridge circulating on the roof perimeter. The platform is supported in regular vertical intervals by guiding eyes that are fastened onto fixing hooks. These hooks are located inside the fish mouth and are thus invisible from the outside, enhancing the smooth uniform appearance of the façade.

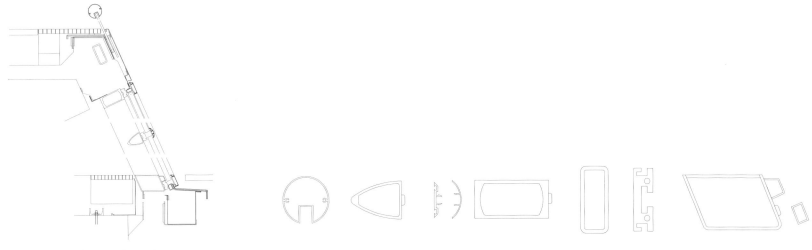

Basement (M 1:25), profiles (M 1:7,5)

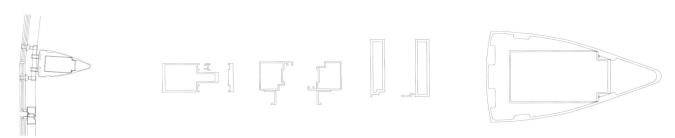

Façade ground floor (M 1:25), profiles (M 1:7,5)

Façade elevator tower (M 1:25), profiles (M 1:7,5)

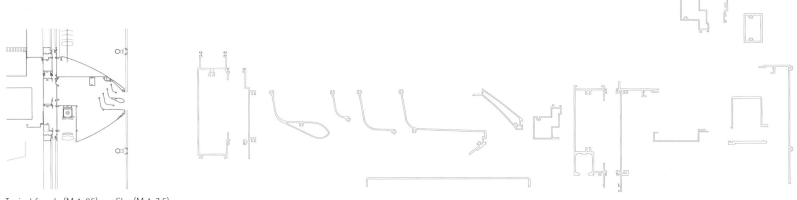

Typical façade (M 1:25), profiles (M 1:7,5)

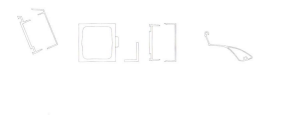

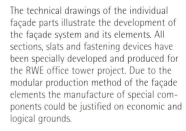

The technical drawings of the individual façade parts illustrate the development of the façade system and its elements. All sections, slats and fastening devices have been specially developed and produced for the RWE office tower project. Due to the modular production method of the façade elements the manufacture of special components could be justified on economic and logical grounds.

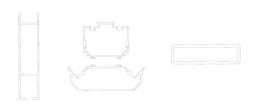
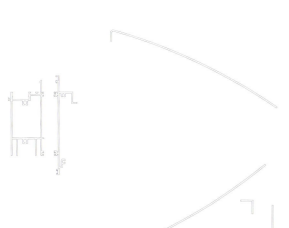
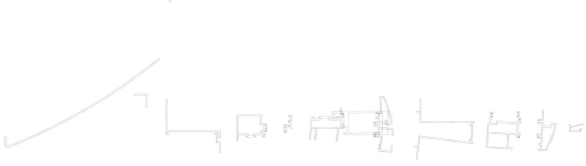

Façade patterns and tests

When designing large façades, it is customary nowadays to conduct tests on original parts. The size of the test area usually comprises several modules and extends over two or three floors. As tests of this magnitude can normally not be conducted inside a building, they mostly take place at outside tests sites, with the added benefit that the façade can be tested under both inside and outside conditions. In these tests a full-scale part of the façade is erected in front of a stabilised wall, with original fittings and in exactly the same way as it will later be erected on site. The façade edges are then fixed to the wall and the whole construct is sealed to create an air-tight space between wall and façade. This void is connected to a fan that is used to create positive or negative differential pressures to the ambient pressure. Furthermore, a water jet system is installed in front of the façade that simulates strong rainfall. Using this test arrangement, the façade is then tested for air and water tightness to 20% of maximum design load and for stability of all parts to 150% of maximum design loads. In addition to these standard tests, this extraordinary project, which is no less than a pioneering undertaking in high-rise construction, calls for special tests where the suitability of the façade for its intended application can be fully examined.

For this purpose, a similar test chamber was installed on top of an existing building, around 20 metres above ground. The inner glass wall of the test façade was fitted with a door that was kept open with a set force of 120 N. Temperature sensors were fitted across the entire height of the façade corridor. The testers then proceeded to measure the air speed at the point of entry on the outer glass wall and 0.5 metres behind the opening. Using a test gas to display the level of decrease in concentration, the air change rate was established. All test data were simultaneously and automatically recorded throughout one year. Thunder storms as well as spring and autumn winds 'simulated' weather conditions high-rise buildings are typically exposed to. The following test results were particularly pertinent:

· To what extent does direct sunlight cause a rise in temperature inside the façade corridor? Test result: a maximum of 6°C; it must be noted here that this effect only lasts for 2 hours;
· What happens in high winds? Test result: Not much! The air speed measured at 0.5 metres behind the 'door' remained below 0.5 m/s. The force exerted on the closing-edge of the door remained below 120 N. Rain does not travel into the incoming air vents!
· What is the air change rate? Test result: According to the diagram and depending on wind speed and

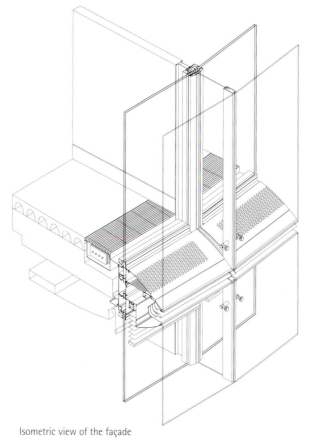

Isometric view of the façade

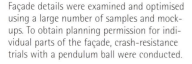

Façade details were examined and optimised using a large number of samples and mockups. To obtain planning permission for individual parts of the façade, crash-resistance trials with a pendulum ball were conducted.

The precise design and surface characteristics of the glass pane fasteners and glass prints were developed on several 1:1 models.

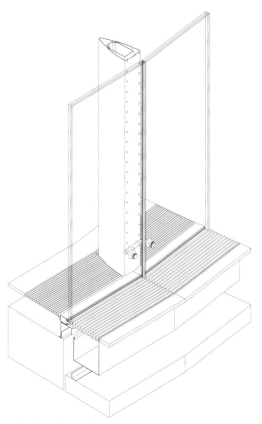

Isometric view of ground floor façade element

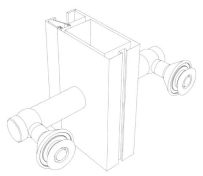

Isometric view of the window pane fastening device.

The ground floor façade features full-height (4.20 m) glazing, vertically divided into two halves. The air supply for the screening of cold incoming air run inside the – structurally required – hollow sections; air is blown through vents directed at the glass pane.

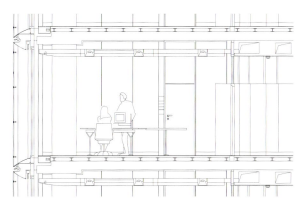

The mock-up of the point where four façade elements meet, showing the relevant corners of each façade element.

ambient temperature the air change rate was found to be between x 2 and x 10; the positive experiences of the occupants later confirm the test results.
· Is the formation of icicles in the vicinity of air extraction vents possible?

In order to achieve short installation paths, the main air-technical installations unit was to be located at the building's centre of gravity. The humid extracted air produced by the air conditioning therefore exits in the immediate vicinity of the façade. When using conventional outlet vent grids the air speed is too low and condensation occurs on the outlet slats, forming dangerous icicles in winter. The problem was avoided by designing nozzle outlets out of which air exits sufficiently fast so that it mixes quickly with the dry outside air and condensation is prevented.

The supply and extracted air vents were optimised once a series of elaborate aerodynamic examinations on sample elements had provided enough data.

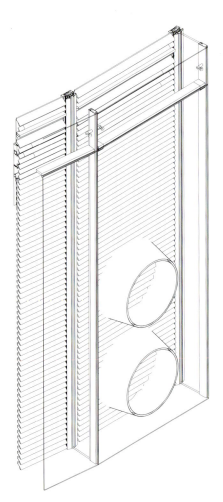

Isometric view of façade element, technical installations floor

Manufacture and installation

In the interest of optimising the construction and design, existing sections were disregarded and a completely new set of sections was designed and manufactured. Digitally operated tooling machines with a precision of +/- 0.1 mm were employed for the manufacture of the sections. The façade is structured into a grid of horizontal ring elements each 2 metres apart; the inner façade also has a vertical division where fixed and sliding window panes meet. When the sliding window is opened it slides along the inside of the fixed pane; when the sliding window is closed, a special fitting presses the window forward so it closes flush with the fixed pane and is locked all around the edge, thus providing the necessary seal. Operation via a hand wheel ensures fine-adjustment of the opening, which for safety reasons is limited to 13 cm. The outer façade elements are connected to the inner façade elements with double cantilever arms. The fish mouth fitted with vents is manufactured in parts; its curious shape only appears when assembled. The frames of the inner and outer façade elements, including window panes and glass, are made at the factory. The glass panes of the outer façade are fixed to eight fastening devices. These are carefully calculated bearings that accommodate expansion forces and tolerances; this enables the fastening devices to be completely flexible: they can move in any direction. These fastening characteristics were imperative due to the brittleness of the pre-tensioned glass and they were also a precondition for special building permission.

The installation of the façade was considerably facilitated due to the high degree of pre-fabrication. First, fastening anchors were fitted. Shell-related tolerances in all three axes have been carefully corrected to the exact theoretically required value. This work was carried out without rush, long before the installation of the façade elements. The assembled elements were then delivered to the site on customised transport frames in bundles of three units each and hoisted onto platforms with a crane, from where they were distributed on the respective floors. Hoisting the element bundles took no time at all and did not require precision. The position of the platforms was offset every 6 to 8 floors. A crane trolley running in an overhead track was used to hang the elements into position. The elements were handled from the ceiling and taken to the exact place of installation with the monorail system.

Thanks to high-precision manufacture the actual process of fitting was merely a matter of minutes. As soon as an element was in place the façade was weatherproof at that particular point. Further sealing processes are not required with this type of construction.

The final installation stage comprised the fitting of ceiling and wall connections. At times, the installation work outlined above had to be carried out in severe winter weather conditions in order to finish construction on time.

Construction and façade of the elevator shaft

The elevator shaft is a light-weight steel frame construction which adopts full storey-height glazing and slatted sun blinds from the main façade. The unrestricted view is maintained. The steel frame was assembled with the same tight tolerances of the main façade. The elevator rails are fastened to the steel frame. The elevator tower comprises a centrally placed concrete slab – effectively an extension of the main building's storey ceiling – to form the front-of-elevator access zone, and twin U-shaped elevator shafts; they were completely pre-fabricated and were delivered and hoisted fully assembled. Savings were thus made in scaffolding costs and installation time.

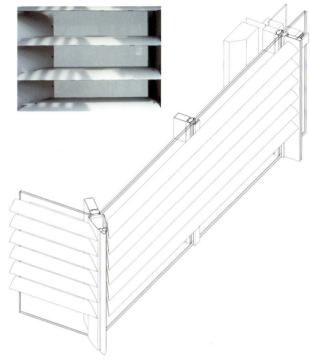

Isometric view of the slats on the elevator tower façade

This photo sequence shows the manufacture of the façade elements, from the production of sections (top row), via the part-assembly in the workshop (rows 2-6) to the finished product. Once complete, the elements were packed and stroed on palettes for transport. Throughout the entire production process Gartner façade specialists examined and tested all planning details as well as the quality of execution – from the sections approved for the façade elements through to the finished element fitted with all components – before giving the all clear for the trial-extrusion of the sections.

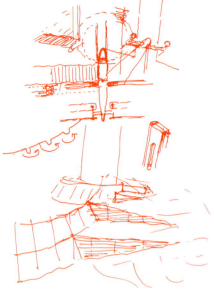

Basement façade / basement

One condition for the transition between the tower and the bottom horizontal block was to keep the circular plans, albeit with offset centres and considerably larger diameters. This initially resulted in a façade surface that was not developable (i. e.: the façade cannot, theoretically, be unfulled flat) and therefore would have required twisted insulation glazing. Slight modifications in the design geometry finally resulted in a building shape similar to a frustum inclined against the vertical plane. This surface is developable, the glass panes remain flat. Nonetheless, the façade includes trapeze-shaped elements of varying sizes and angles. Partition walls are connected via crooked adapter pieces. The clear geometry of the frustum enables the creation of a dimension calculation programme for all façade elements and glass panes on which precise factory-based assembly is based. A horizontal parapet rail is added to the façade; the glass pane formats are approx. 2.5/3.0. The façade is concluded at the top with an integrated fully glazed railing. The bottom of the façade terminates only a fraction above the level of the lake. It was feared that strong winds might whip large quantities of water against the façade. The solution comprised the installation of a drain as well as the creation of a void inside the façade which is kept at excess pressure by a fan, thus creating a barrier-vacuum. This way, air may leak at several unknown points but water cannot enter.

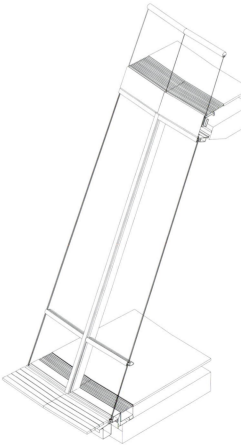

Isometric view of façade, basement

The geometry of the basement façade corresponds to the rolled out surface of a frustum, resulting in a different pane shape for each window. The various glass panes were lowered into their fastenings with a special crane.

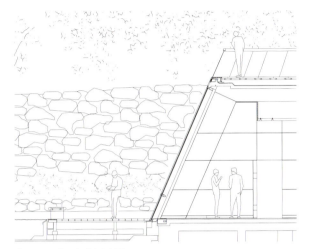
Basement façade (M 1:140)

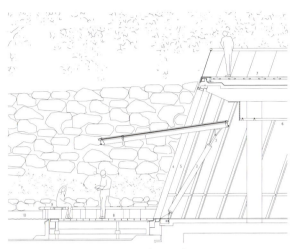
Basement façade with raising gate (M 1:140)

For the casino in the basement three emergency exits were required. As the façade was inclined throughout, the necessary addition of wind-protector portals for the emergency doors would have prevented an efficient use of space and impaired the appearance of the façade considerably. The restrictions led us to the concept of four by four metre vertically inclined gates, angular in plan. The gate opens around a horizontal axis at about two-thirds of its height. When open, the gates reveal a wide and direct exit to the terrace in front while at the same time providing a roof above the exit. We managed to find a position for the gates that accommodated the spatial angularity caused by the contours of the façade.

The gates are operated by twin pneumatic cylinders that are pre-tensioned with springs so that the gates can be opened automatically even in case of power failure.

To prevent lake water from leaking through the gates, they are sated with the excess pressure barrier system outlined above.

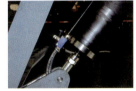
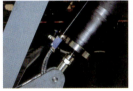

The final design of the raising gates that form part of the basement façade were finally approved by Gartner after many meticulous performance tests. The gates are operated hydraulically; springs inside the pistons provide sufficient pre-tension to ensure that the gates can still be operated manually in case of a power cut.

Engineering Concept
Tony McLaughlin

The ideas for the technical systems for the RWE tower were developed on the basis of experiences made during the Commerzbank competition project which Ingenhoven and Partners had participated in a few months previously. Form the outset, the conventional approach to services in a high-rise building were put into question. Why, for example, should a façade be completely sealed if an appropriate construction would enable occupants to open the windows, weather permitting, in order to naturally ventilate the building? Or, why should systems with a variable air volume be the accepted standard for high-quality offices?

The aim of the project team, then, was to create a high-quality building incorporating all modern and applicable methods for the regulation of the internal climate, such as thermal mass, forced (suction) and nocturnal ventilation, etc. Methods like these had already been employed successfully, but not necessarily in high buildings and only in combination with conventional façades.

At the same time, this building was to be a low energy consumer. One of the principal aims was to drastically reduce energy requirements compared to conventional office towers housing a large corporation's headquarters. In order to present our vision we drew up a diagram, similar to a cooking recipe. In this diagram, similar to a construction schedule, we listed all the fundamental points that needed to be examined.

The primary office environment, which provided the unique opportunity to introduce elements such as 'cooled girders and façade elements' due to its predominantly cellular structure, was at the centre of our contemplations. Large open-plan offices would have presented us with more complex problems with regards to heat and light regulation; we would have had to compromise in our attempts to introduce advanced systems for the regulation of environmental parameters. Early on we concentrated on cooled girders and on the integration of ceiling elements that were to be suspended from a concrete skeleton. The cooled girder elements were also to accommodate office lighting, sprinkler system and fire alarms. The accommodation of fresh air supply, low voltage electricity supply and IT and communication lines was to be housed in a double-floor cavity, envisaged at that stage to be 300 mm high. Both services zones were to be fed via supply rings in the circular corridor zone.

Although cooled girders were always the team's premier option, the performance of other systems was nonetheless examined in a study, for example:
· cooled girders with mechanical ventilation
· cooled ceilings with mechanical ventilation
· an induction system mounted inside the ceiling
· a total air-VAV-system.

In a parallel energy technology study, the above mentioned technical systems were tested in combination with various types of façade.

The client then commissioned UE Consult with the scientific calculations on the basis of the concept developed by the team, whereby the properties of the façade systems and the environmental systems in particular were to be investigated on thermal models.

The following diagrams show the initial results of UE Consult deliberations; alongside a 'contentment matrix', these results encouraged the team to pursue the idea of a naturally ventilated façade with cooled girders and mechanical ventilation.

After the team had opted for the cooled girders they began to concentrate their design efforts on aesthetic aspects and integration into the office world. Parallel to the environmental examinations, the concrete skeleton emerged as a winning solution as it not only provided excellent structural efficiency but also allowed the amount of the exposed thermal mass of the concrete intrados to be increased, with all efforts geared towards a vaulted contour tapering towards the windows.

It now emerged that the cavity of the vaulted intrados could quite naturally accommodate not only the cooled girders but also other services equipment that needed to run inside the ceiling, such as lighting, sprinklers, fire alarms and sound absorption devices. What emerged was a largely integrated arrangement that, thanks to its shape, the team labelled the 'surfboard'. Within this arrangement, the cooled girder was redesigned to look like a finned cage with cooling water running through it. The air in the rooms could there-

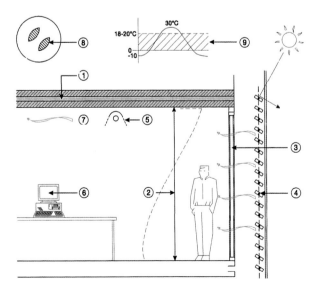

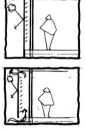

1. Exposed thermal mass – resists changes in building temperature, stores energy from cool night air, radiates coolth to occupied space during day time.
2. Height – allows stratification of room air and increases allowable temperature differential between supply and exhaust air.
3. Solar controlling glazing – low solar gain, low heat loss – good daylight.
4. Good quality shading – reduce solar gains to a minimum whilst maintaining visual outside contact.
5. Limit artificial lighting – use energy efficient light source (12 w/m target) and link to daylight levels, incorporate measures to improve day lighting.
6. Limit equipment gains – override central equipment rooms.
7. Remove exhaust air from highest points in the rooms.
8. Thermal mass in the core of the building.
9. Take advantage of 'free cooling'.

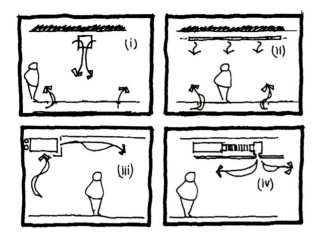

1. Chilled beam with displacement air
2. Chilled ceiling with displacement air
3. Ceiling mounted induction system
4. VAV air system

fore circulate freely around the 'surfboard' and thus provide the necessary cooling for the offices. Due to the finned surface of the cooling elements the heat exchange was effectuated predominantly by convection, a fact that led to discussions within the team with regards to the potential interaction of convection with the upwards current inside the offices.

After all, we were dealing with a special, customised, universally applicable ceiling element whose performance needed to be examined and tested to ensure that the design criteria – performance and comfort – were met. The client asked the internationally renowned company Trox, with their vast experience in the field of heating and cooling equipment manufacture, to conduct these tests.

The 'surfboard' as a cooled girder was, however, only to be deployed in the floors leading up to the technical installations floor, i.e. the office floors only. The application of the cooled girders did not appear appropriate in the floors above, as the cooling load is much higher there and the use of these rooms is very mixed indeed (e.g. dining rooms, conference rooms, etc.). But the principle of the (ceiling-) integrated 'surfboard' was applied, i.e. the ducts and diffusers were integrated into the same form, albeit not finned.

On a more comprehensive level, the technical systems of the tower were developed around the principle that the cooling equipment, heat source (fed by the city's district heating supply), the power supply, main electrical distribution units, water supply and sprinkler reservoirs would be located in the basement while the majority of supply and extracted air equipment would be located with the heat rejection equipment on the 18th floor.

A circular building is very efficient as far as the façade or energy requirements are concerned, but interesting problems arise, for example, in the area of services equipment. A strategy was devised placing the electricity and water supplies into two main riser shafts inside the stairwell cores and the ducts for vertical air distribution into the tower's inner core. At floor level, the air supply ducts branch out into a storey-wide network inside the cavity of the raised floor while the extracted air – air extraction was to occur just below the ceilings of all offices located at the building's perimeter – flows through ducts inside the cavity of the drop ceiling in the corridor where, incidentally, the cold water pipes are located as well.

The offices are heated by a convector heating system, located at the building's perimeter and supplied via risers placed at the two stairwell cores' perimeters.

From the outset, this was to be a building fitted with perfectly co-ordinated services equipment with a high degree of variability. Every element was to be adjusted and optimised for use, which in some places required a high degree of inventiveness due to very specific equipment installation arrangements.

One example is the development of the smoke extraction system for the restaurant on level -1. The point of departure was the proposal by the Happort office to use large skylights, operated via pistons, that would open in case of fire. This proposal was further developed into the large gates, functioning not only as smoke extractors but at the same time as emergency access to the outside.

By the same token, concepts were devised to adopt the 'surfboard's' 'restrained aesthetic' that was applied in the offices for the larger public areas. Part of this concept is the visible finned surface of the concrete construction. The public areas are heated/cooled via an air system, which required the ducts that supplied the ceiling elements to be embedded into the ceiling's concrete structure. The cooling air flowing through the ducts cool the concrete mass and therefore contribute to stable ambient conditions in the room. The grid of smaller air ducts branch off the main supply ducts located in the core zone. The concept sketch shows the extent of required co-ordination.

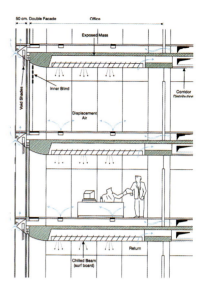

Typical section (M 1:160) showing the thermal mass of the concrete ceilings and of the technical element integrated into the ceiling vault ('surfboard').

Testing the 'surfboard's' performance at TGT-Krantz in Bergisch-Gladbach.

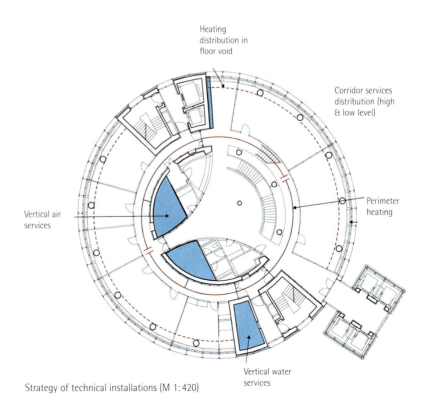

Strategy of technical installations (M 1:420)

Air
Joachim Stoll

For the RWE tower in Essen, detailed air flow simulator tests were conducted to examine all aspects of natural ventilation in relation to the double-layer façade which was used here for the first time. The following issues were analysed in detail, particularly with regards to effects typical in high-rise construction:
· natural ventilation in windy conditions
· natural vertical thermal ventilation of the entire building
· ventilation and warming in the double-layer façade
· ventilation and warming in the elevator tower
· natural ventilation of the ventilation duct network

1. Wind
Wind can have varying effects on a building, for example the destruction of externally mounted sun screens, cross-ventilation from windward side to lee, increased air flow speeds through doorways and in corridors, increased air flow speeds in the offices, increased door opening forces, etc.

1.1. Wind conditions on site
In Essen, south to westerly winds prevail. Wind speeds around the upper floors of the building are, taking the building's height and its location within Essen into account, still 30 - 40 % higher than wind speeds around the local weather station.

1.2. Wind forces exerted onto the building, aerodynamics of the building
The following graphs illustrate the different pressure dispersion on the external layer of the building for different oncoming wind directions. Strong suction peaks, caused by the air flow around cylindrical buildings (and also known from aircraft wings) are clearly visible on the charts.

1.3. Weather-proof sun screens
The wind shield created by the double-layer façade allows the integration of sun screens that are not exposed to weather conditions and therefore allow for further optimisation with regards to the slatted surface. The stored heat generated by the integrated sun screens is sufficiently extracted, so that the total energy transmission rate typical for summer sunlight can be limited to around 10-12%, which is equivalent to the screening achieved by externally mounted sun protection, in other words in physical terms an excellent result. Typical neutral sun-protection-glazing is far less effective with energy transmission rates of around 30-40%. Thanks to the double-layered façade the cooling loads during the summer months and the required cooling surfaces on the ceiling can be dramatically reduced, in turn allowing parts of the ceiling to be activated for thermal storage and thus reducing costs considerably.

1.4. Equalising wind pressure
In an initial attempt, a concept to equalise wind pressure inside a circular double-layered façade was developed which would have been very effective in achieving comparable pressures in the two building parts separated by the stairwells. However, increased acoustic demands with regards to potential sound transmission within the façade corridor made it impossible to continue developing this concept for the RWE tower.

2. Natural ventilation of all floors
An individual ventilation by opening the windows was always envisaged for psychological reasons, in order to achieve a high level of employee satisfaction and to reduce energy costs. Here, the double-layer façade offers the advantage of limited dynamic wind impact on the offices. Measurements at the Gartner façade test site have shown a reasonable air change rate produced by the perpetually changing wind pressures. Within the context of our air flow simulator tests, outlined below, the possibilities offered by the double-layered façade with regards to a minimisation of cross-ventilation and door opening forces were further examined.

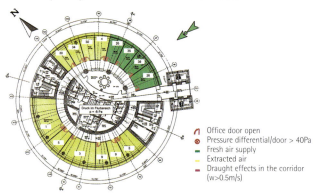

Air exchange at medium wind speeds (4m/s)

2.1. Cross-ventilation
The following graph shows the typical ventilation throughout the building at medium wind speeds with opened windows and doors in the offices and up to a 40-fold air change rate; the slits in the double-layer façade provide a sufficient reduction of cross-ventilation and effectively help prevent the flying about of loose paper.

2.2. Door opening forces
Not only cross-ventilation but also the occurrence of increased door opening forces and increased forces exerted on partition walls, both caused by the perpetuation of wind pressures inside the building, must be expected; these may have an adverse impact not only on individual ventilation (opening windows) but also on the general operation of the building. According to ergonomic tests, door opening forces of 40-60 N (4-6 kg) are considered comfortable and door opening forces of around 100 N (10 kg) are considered borderline. The next graph shows typical door pressures, at wind

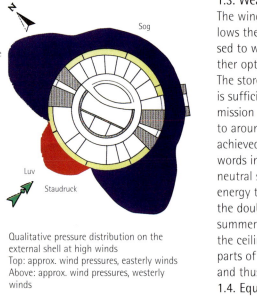

Qualitative pressure distribution on the external shell at high winds
Top: approx. wind pressures, easterly winds
Above: approx. wind pressures, westerly winds

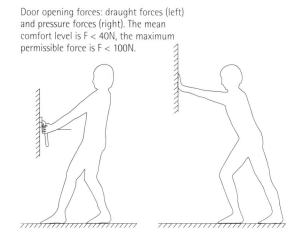

Door opening forces: draught forces (left) and pressure forces (right). The mean comfort level is F < 40N, the maximum permissible force is F < 100N.

speeds of 8 m/s, to be around 50 Pa, equivalent to door opening forces of 50 N (5 kg) for single-hinged doors with a 2m² surface.

2.3. Operational limitations for window-ventilation

The frequent overstepping of the comfort level and even the borderline level of the office air change rate and door opening forces was subsequently examined for several 'opening scenarios', focussing on the ventilation of two simultaneously 'open' offices (1:1) and all offices 'open' at the same time (1:n). The deviations of the two scenarios were relatively low, so that results could be easily interpreted. During c. 30-40 % of operating time the air change rate is more than 25-fold, a point at

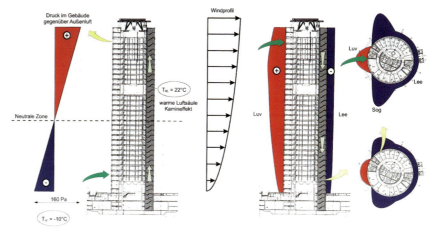

Driving forces in the vertical air streams throughout the building:
Left: thermics, upward air streams
Right: wind, up- and downward air streams

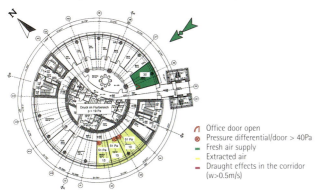

Pressure on doors at high wind speeds (8m/s)

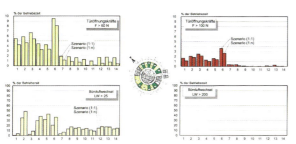

A reduction of comfort levels and operating restrictions in case of wind providing natural ventilation.

which closing the office doors is recommended. A c. 200-fold air change, when loose paper would be expected to fly about in a building with this type of double-layered façade, is prevented by the sectional limitations produced by the vents. However, door opening forces in some – particularly western - offices exceed the comfort level for 5% of operating time and the borderline level for 2% of operating time, which leads to the conclusion that the double-layer façade is not able to prevent increased door opening forces in all places at all times. This led to the development of the control panels mounted in every office (see illustration); the building 'communicates' with the occupants via the control panels by indicating whether windows can currently be opened or not. When wind speeds reach c. 8 m/s, which happens on average around 300 hours per annum, the control panel indicates that windows must be closed.

3. Natural vertical ventilation throughout the building

3.1. Propelling forces

Apart from possible differences in wind pressure on the various floors, the natural vertical ventilation throughout the building is predominantly propelled by the building's thermal conditions, i.e. the elevator and stairwell shafts' 'chimney effect' (see ill.). Therefore, there is excess atmospheric pressure in the upper floors and low atmospheric pressure in the lower floors. The area of equal atmospheric pressure (i.e. the same inside as outside) is known as the neutral zone.

3.2. Elevators and stairwells

The RWE headquarters tower has
· 4 glass elevators in the elevator shaft
· 2 fire brigade elevators/express elevators inside the building and
· 2 stairwells inside the building
all of them located inside shafts reaching from level -3 to 27.

3.3. Smoke extractor and pressure regulator flaps, engine rooms

As the following illustrations show, it was crucial to keep the smoke extractor flaps inside the elevator shafts and

Below left: natural ventilation throughout the building with windows closed; effect of smoke extractor vents in the elevator shafts, smoke extractor vents open and closed.
Below right: natural ventilation throughout the building with windows closed; effect of pressure stabiliser flaps, pressure stabiliser flaps open and closed.

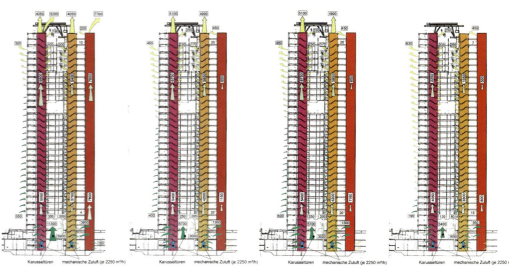

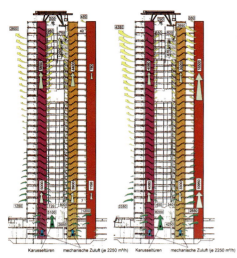

Natural ventilation throughout the building with windows open; effect of the air locks in the glass elevator tower (per storey 1 office with the window and the door open)
Left: air locks closed
Right: air locks open

the pressure regulator flaps in the stairwell shafts closed to avoid cold air coming in via the entrance areas. Since lift force caused by low outside temperatures would have caused conventional pressure regulator flaps to open, we decided to install remote-controlled pressure regulator flaps in this building.

3.4. Elevator doors, air locks

Because the elevator doors are not completely airtight the architects planned air lock doors in front of the elevator doors in an attempt to reduce vertical ventilation throughout the building. The effect of the air lock doors can be seen using an example where office windows and doors are open, along with the resultant air volume flow in the elevator shafts. The significance of the air lock doors is further illustrated by the high air volume flow on the ground floor and level -1, which is connected to the ground floor via the lobby, as air lock doors have not been installed in this area.

3.5. Lobby, terrace doors

The lobby area required special attention due to the external doors and the fact that the elevators link the lobby with a large number of floors. Within the context of fine-adjustments to air flow resistance within the buil-ding, measures to improve airtightness of
· revolving lobby doors
· stairwell air lock doors on levels -1 to -3 and
· entrance air locks to the underground parking on levels -1 and -2 were taken.

Furthermore, recommendations could be derived with regards to the airtightness of the hydraulic lift from level -3 to level 0 and preventing the opening of the terrace doors on levels -1 and 27 during the winter months.

3.6. Office ventilation by opening windows

The effects of natural vertical ventilation on office window-ventilation are moderate. The office doors are very airtight, so that with office doors closed and windows open cross-ventilation remains below a 20-fold air change rate; with the doors open it increases to a 70-fold air change rate, which is still not sufficient to cause loose paper to fly about. The intensity of the ventilation can, of course, be easily reduced by closing individual office doors. Air speeds up to 0.3 m/s are possible within this scenario, but this was considered acceptable if it only occurred for a short time.

3.7. Door opening forces, elevator shaft doors

Given the overall height of the RWE tower and the position of the neutral pressure zone, it was recommended that windows are only opened when outside temperatures are above +2°C, in order to avoid door opening forces higher than 100 N (10 kg). Furthermore, the pressure differences around the elevator shaft doors were calculated and relevant guidelines were transmitted to the elevator manufacturer.

4. Natural ventilation inside the façade and elevator tower

In order to minimise any further operational limitations in office ventilation by opening windows, summer warming needed to be reduced in the double-layer façade. Still with regards to summer warming, particular attention needed to be directed towards the elevator tower as well.

4.1. The double-layer façade

The next illustration shows the expected air temperatures inside the façade corridor for the two building segments (NE and SW) separated by the two stairwells. On the left, the conditions on a sunny July day are shown; on the right, the frequency of higher temperatures occurring in an average year is shown. Due to a combination of exposure to intense sunshine and higher afternoon temperatures, peak temperatures of 42-45°C have been calculated for the western façade. These temperatures could be reduced more effectively by installing larger vents in the external layer, but for this building the peak temperatures were considered

Air temperature inside the double-layer façade
Left: course of a sunny July day, according to DIN 4710/VDI 2078
Right: course of one year for the trial reference year TRY region 3

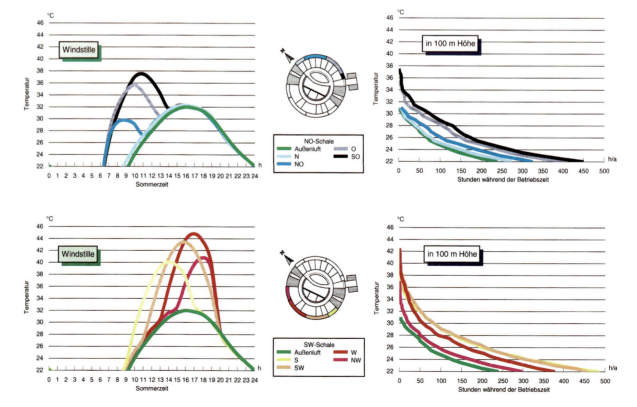

acceptable as they help reduce cross-ventilation (as outlined above). Extremely high temperatures have a relatively low incidence anyway: depending on the orientation of the façade, temperatures above 25°C occur for about 100-250 hours per annum.

4.2. Elevator tower

For the elevator tower, several façade options were considered (single or insulation glazing with or without external sun screens). Initial solar ray absorption tests showed that without sun screens and despite the virtually fully glazed elevators, c. 75% of incoming solar rays are absorbed and converted into heat.

It was found that the aerodynamically effective sections for natural ventilation of the elevator tower, taking into consideration the sectional reduction in the area of the elevator cabin, were c. 2m³. In case of single glazing with sun screens the air temperatures in the upper part of the elevator could be reduced from 60°C to 45°C; the actual surfaces, however, remained much warmer. After long deliberations, also considering the winter months, we opted for insulation glazing with external sun screens, which would dramatically reduce solar heat input; furthermore, the natural nocturnal air flow could be mechanically extracted towards the top of the elevator tower.

5. Natural ventilation of the air duct network

Finally, the effects of natural window-ventilation on the operation of the air conditioning equipment were examined. Particular attention was directed towards air supply disparities due to deviations from target-volume-flow. In case of vastly differing wind pressures, reverse air currents and the danger of odour transmission from one office to another must be expected.

5.1. Segmentation of the air duct network

Following initial examinations on the effects of different wind pressures in different floors, the air duct network was segmented to the effect that every floor was equipped with separate air volume flow regulators, and air supply was divided into two zones corresponding to the two façade segments divided by the stairwells (NE and SW segments); see illustration.

5.2. Operational conditions, scenarios

For the remaining inter-linked areas, different scenarios had to be examined with regards to

· mechanical ventilation
· natural ventilation with closed office door and
· natural ventilation with open office door.

5.3. Air flow disparities, reverse air flow

In the following diagram, showing typical target air volume flow for the eastern (NE) façade segment, the dangers of reverse air flow and odour transmission into other offices at 6 m/s wind speed for a windward office with window ventilation are clearly evident. In order to minimise these effects, air flow resistors were adjusted accordingly, thereby effectively preventing reverse air flow even with opened windows, i.e. with wind speeds below 8 m/s. Further restrictions to office window-ventilation with simultaneous mechanical ventilation do not occur.

6. Summary

Thanks to the executed air flow simulator tests, in which
· natural ventilation of individual floors
· natural vertical ventilation of the entire building
· natural ventilation of the double-layer facade
· natural ventilation of the elevator tower
· natural ventilation of the air duct network were closely examined, and further thanks to the thermal simulator tests with respect to the façade and the elevator tower, the operational possibilities and restrictions of window-ventilation could be detected during planning and optimised accordingly in order to design an office building where natural ventilation via the opening of office windows is possible for most of the year. The remaining operational restrictions for office window-ventilation due to
· wind speeds above 8 m/s (c. 300 hours per annum) and
· outside temperatures below +2°C (c. 100-250 hours per annum)
will, during the building's normal operation, be communicated via the control panel to the occupants, who will act accordingly; indeed, different kinds of restrictions will be communicated for each floor. Occupants will react individually on increased temperatures due in the façade corridor to intense summer sunshine.

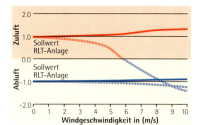

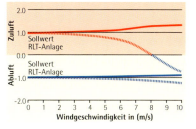

Top: graph illustrating the effect of natural ventilation on the air conditioning system; Bottom: graph illustrating conditions with adjusted settings for air stream resistors; The broken lines represent the rates in a windward office with the window open.

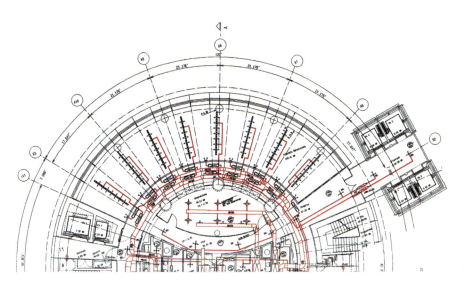

This detail of the reflected ceiling plan shows the arrangement of duct components 'fresh/extracted air' in relation to pressure-loss on individual floors.

Facility Management
Klaus Daniels and
Dieter Henze

Wind tunnel investigations
The buildings and green spaces to be built within the development of the former Stern Brewery site, along with the integration of these green spaces and the existing public city parks, are expected to cause changes in the wind field on the site and in the adjacent urban zones. This applies to the field of pollution (plus traffic) as well as to the wind field near ground level. Furthermore, reference data on the distribution of wind pressures on the building were required to safeguard the aerodynamic simulations, resulting in the IFI (Institut für Industrieaerodynamik GmbH) being commissioned with a comprehensive wind tunnel investigation. The extent of the investigations were specified in a brief authored by the planners and comprised the following problem areas:
· Investigation of the wind field near ground level
· Investigation of the field of pollution
· Ascertaining the wind loads of the building
· Investigation of supply and extracted air
· Investigation of the field of pollution on the roof terrace caused by extracted air flow
· Investigation of ventilation and smoke extraction in a given storey

At a surprisingly early stage, the results of the wind tunnel tests provided essential data for the parameters of the expected wind impact and led to optimised system solutions in the general architecture as well as the technical installations and the calculation of structural elements.

The investigations to ascertain the fields of pollution, the wind fields near ground level and the wind profile on site were conducted on a 1:500 topographic model of the city in a boundary layer wind tunnel; the investigation to ascertain the wind loads, ventilation and smoke extraction data were conducted on a 1:64 sectional model in a free jet wind tunnel.

Elevators
The selection of the precise site for development was based on building regulation issues, structural considerations and, above all, organisational aspects. The fully glazed elevator tower has been placed directly outside the main body of the office tower, thereby serving as a point of orientation with non-intersected front-of-elevator zones for the occupants. The fire fighting elevators in the outer core come in two varieties: goods lift and executive elevator. The resultant reduction of the inner core has led to an optimisation in the ratio of naturally ventilated and lit surfaces to inner auxiliary surfaces.

Two hydraulic glass elevators serve the underground levels with access to the underground parking and the entrance level. The upper floors are served by 4 Thyssen cable elevators with a 13-person capacity each, all four elevators serving all 32 floors. The optimised capacity achievable at a speed of 3.5 m/s is controlled by a combined group control unit which can be switched to one predominant direction for peak charging or discharging periods. The elevators are powered by direct current engines without transmission, fitted with a static converter and mounted in the engine room underneath the top of the building. Thermic simulations to ascertain the expected temperature conditions within the elevator tower led to the elevator being heated during winter and the elevator cabins being cooled during summer with so-called split-devices running at 2 kW per cabin. To reduce warming inside the elevator shaft during summer, openings have been installed in the bottom and extractor vents at the top. In the transitional periods of the year solar heat is used to maintain a steady temperature in the shaft and the front-of-elevator areas. In

Left: external elevator tower, for the vertical dispersion of the building's occupants; 4 elevators with a 13-person-capacity each, speed: 3.5 m/s.
Right: Direct current driven, transmission-free elevator engines in the engine room underneath the building's top.

Wind tunnel models, from left to right: topographical city model 1:500, for examination of wind field near ground level.
Building-top models, for examination of pollution fields on the roof terrace due to extracted air streams.
Section model 1:64 in the free jet wind tunnel, for examination of wind loads due to air streams throughout the building/smoke extraction.

order to counteract thermic lift in winter, the shaft doors and cable guides were completely sealed, so that any influx of cold air from the ground floor and any acoustic nuisance could be minimised.

Photovoltaic elements on the loggia roof

In an attempt to actively tap solar energy, the entrance roof was conceived as a multi-functional unit. Optimisation efforts eventually led to a roof construction with integrated photovoltaic elements. The elements generate electricity and provide shade for the entrance area. Furthermore, the roof forms a visual link with the peripheral buildings extending to both sides of the tower.

192 fish-belly sun-protector slats are integrated into the loggia roof at an angle of 32°; the slats' upper surface is fitted with mono-crystal solar cells. The photovoltaicly generated energy is fed directly into the building's internal grid via a change-over switch. The maximum output is c. 19 kWp. For permanent monitoring of ambient conditions external sensors have been fitted to record
· current horizontal solar radiation
· the generator's current output
· current ambient temperature
· current module temperature and
· energy generated so far.
The data is transmitted via computer to a display panel in the lobby on level -1

Left: the loggia above the main entrance, with integrated photovoltaic cells for the generation of electricity from solar energy.

Heating

The heating in the office tower as well as in the peripheral buildings is supplied by the district heating network of the city of Essen (STEAG); heating supply is indirect via three district heating transfer points.

Considering the required guarantee-data, the building structure and the demand points to be supplied, the additional heat generation stands at 2900 kW.

To separate the city's primary grid from the internal secondary grid, the following heat exchangers have been installed, given a simultaneity of 0.9:
· 2 heat exchangers, 1300 kW each – stat. and dyn.heating
· 1 heat exchanger 120 kW – outside heating/driveway
· 1 heat exchanger 50 kW – warm water generation kitchen/recreation rooms.

To create an economic pressure level, separate pressure zones are envisaged, secured by plate-type heat exchangers.

Distribution of heating water is effectuated in a two-pipe system from the central transfer unit on the 3rd floor via pumps (pressure differential-controlled) to the central climate control-units on level -3 and to the technical installations floor (T1) in the tower. The heat exchangers for the pressure zones 1 and 2 are installed in the technical installations floor alongside the distributors/reservoirs. The heating circuits were divided into main consumer circuits, according to demand point structure and building configuration as well as pressure zone arrangements.

Warm water generation

After deliberations as to the building's economic balance it was decided that decentralised warm water generation via small built-in electric boiler units represented the most economical solution. Central warm water generation was only required for the kitchens and recreation rooms on the underground levels, via a warm water reservoir, heated indirectly by a heat exchanger with a heating-up period of 2 hours and a power rating of 50 kW.

Outside heating

To ensure that the driveway remains frost-free the drive-way ramps and the driveway itself are heated by a water-filled underfloor heating system. The water is heated by a plate-type water exchanger installed in the STEAG transfer room on level -1.

To prevent corrosion within the pipe network and to stabilise hardness, appropriate softener and dosage devices have been installed in the feeder pipe of the system.

Regulation and control

An electronic regulation system (DDC) that is connected to the building's central control unit regulates and controls the heating installations. The office heating system is integrated into the heating surface control via the overriding BUS-system. For the control circuits of the static heating system, weather-dependant control units with day/night and weekly settings have been installed. The pre-heaters of the RLT-aggregates have been fitted with a constant temperature control in the flow pipes.

Heating surfaces

The heating surfaces have been selected within the context of structural and architectural parameters and corresponding to the façade grid system;
· flat radiators with a smooth front in one or multi layered versions for auxiliary rooms, toilets, external elevator
· floor-level convector heaters for the offices, staff restaurants, external front-of-elevator areas as well as stairwells T1, T2 and ground floor
· underfloor heating on the ground floor and ground floor lobby as well as driveway ramp and door curtain of the delivery access on level -1.

Every radiator is fitted with a thermostat in the flow connection; in the return connection they are fitted with a control screw, stop and evacuation valves as well as an air evacuation valve. To avoid cold air building up around the high glass façade in the lobby, an air-filled heating system was installed, in which warm air is blown onto the glass panes via static façade sections, preventing condensation. For the glass dome in the boardroom, the construction and the size of the area to be heated necessitated a water-filled section heating system.

Sanitary zones

Waste and rain water from overground floors is discharged via concealed pipe systems directly into the city's sewers. For the underground floors, special pumping devices fitted with backflow barriers pump the waste water into the sewers. Greasy waste water from the kitchens is filtered through a separator and then pumped in the same way.

Central heating unit on level -3 with district heating transfer as an indirect feed into the building via heat exchanger; division into individual pressure zones with pump circuits; controls and safety control panels and, finally, line distributions to the individual demand points.

Water supply

Water is supplied directly from the city's water supply pipes via a connector on level -2. To prevent standing water in the fire fighting pipes, the building's supply pipe is led above the underground parking's fire fighting pipe into the sanitary centre on level -3. The water is fed into the building's pipe network via back-purge filters and a pressure reduction unit.

The pipe configurations are set according to existing demand point structures and the division of pressure zones:
- Main distributor, level -3 sprinkler control unit, recreation rooms, cistern
- via pressure increase distributor for demand points in kitchens;
  demand points, underground levels to 7th floor;
  fire extinguishing, underground levels to 7th floor;
  demand points, substation TO
- via further pressure increase
  demand points, 8th - 27th floor
  fire extinguishing, 8th - 27th floor

The maximum connection rate is 23m^3/h for drinking water and 150m^3/h for fire extinguishing.

For the supply of special water demand points in the kitchens as well as cooling towers, and additional heating supply and air conditioning units, a double water softener has been installed, producing soft water at 3° dH. A reverse-osmosis device is switched in sequence (after the softener) to supply the cold vapour moisturisers of the air conditioning units with the necessary amount of pure water, ensuring trouble-free air conditioning performance. To prevent corrosion damage caused by the rather aggressive soft water, pressure-resistant plastic pipes were used here.

Water installations in the gardens

The landscaping concept – intended to enhance the area around the tower and make full use of adiabatic cooling effects during summer – comprised a variety of water surfaces. The water for the basins, cascades and the lake with a surface of 1,800 m^2 is supplied via a differentiated purification and circulation aggregate on level -3.

A 150m^3-cistern collects unsoiled rain water to supply the gardens' irrigation systems during the summer months.

The detailed planning process revealed that, because the lake surface directly joins the inclined casino glass façade and the terrace, spray and overlapping waves may soil the glass façade and render the terrace unusable. To prevent this from occurring, even in windy conditions, a drain was required. The IFI, Institut für Industrieaerodynamik GmbH, Aachen, devised a system comprising an appropriately dimensioned drain, wind protection measures and subsequent collecting containers that ensures swift and proper draining of lake water even in the worst-case-scenario.

The lake, with adjacent restaurant terrace; the lake surface is c. 1800 m^2, filled with collected rain water. The lake is supplied with recycled and filtered water via a waterfall; the drain is located on the vertical façade of the executive dining rooms.

Fire extinguishing

The first line of fire fighting is ensured by fire extinguishing boxes with steel tube, connected to a wet riser and fire alarm; they are placed throughout the building, incl. underground parking, at the entry to all emergency access routes.

Due to the specific construction of the building with regards to the double-layer façade, the inspecting officer demanded an automatic, blanket-coverage sprinkler system to ensure early fire fighting capabilities that would minimise the risk of a fire spreading. The integration of a sprinkler system enabled the architects to increase the size of fire compartments and to reduce the fire-proofing specifications of individual building parts, thus considerably reducing overall fit-out costs.

The sprinkler system comprises a central water supply with connection to the city's public supply network, a reservoir containing enough water for fire-fighting purposes in case of public water supply breakdown, an air-pressurised water container as a second reserve and, finally, the central pressure-increase pumps.

The pump configuration corresponds to the pressure stages connected to the reserve system. Every sprinkler starts automatically and can only be turned off by hand. The entire pipe network of the wet-sprinkler system is always filled with water and is under permanent excess pressure. If a sprinkler is activated, the pressure at the sprinkler nozzle – and, therefore, in the entire pipe network – drops and the alarm valve station is opened by the water pressure exerted on the distributor. The pressure switch comes into contact with water and thus the fire alarm is activated via the fire detection system.

The sprinkler heads are fitted with a finely toothed deflector and mounted on the ceiling underside, issuing a fine and even spray. In case of fire, only the sprinklers directly above and in the vicinity of the fire will be activated to avoid wide-spread water damage.

Central sprinkler unit on level -1 supplying the building's floors above ground as well as the underground parking, with pressure-increasing pumps, alarm-valve stations and compressed air-water boilers as well as reservoirs.

Climate control-systems, air conditioning

An essential cornerstone of the architects' building concept was the desire to enable the occupants of a building as high as this maximum scope in individually ventilating their work environment during as long a period of the year as possible – this had direct reverberations on the decisions regarding the extent to which climate control installations were to be employed in the building. At the same time, the work spaces should be as pleasant as possible – while energy and hardware requirements necessary to maintain these pleasant conditions should be kept to a minimum. Within the framework of an elaborate theoretical and experimental optimisation process – based on a finely-balanced, comprehensive concept for building shape, façade and technical equipment – the planners arrived at a customised solution which enabled the occupants of the offices to enjoy natural ventilation for 70-80% of the time they spent in the building. By activating the building's [thermic] storage capacities, in combination with a potential night-time cooling-off period made possible by the insulating properties of the double-layer façade, the expected energy requirements of the building were 25% lower than those of a conventionally air conditioned building. During periods when ventilation via the windows is not recommended for energy, safety or comfort reasons, the necessary supply of fresh outside air with a 2.5-fold air change is ensured by a supporting air supply and extraction system capable of heat recycling, cooling and moisturising. Thermic loads during the summer are discharged via convective cooling elements integrated into the office ceilings. Through the efforts by all the planners, at a very early stage, in optimising the building concept, interesting ecological and economical synergies could be achieved, where the façade – in combination with supportive structural and technical measures – enables individual contact to the outside world while at the same time protecting the interior from negative influences of the outside climate and allowing the occupants to benefit from positive outside influences when appropriate. To maintain the comfortable and pleasant conditions in the offices and to optimise energy-use, an intelligent control system was devised that allows occupants to control and adjust functions – such as activating/deactivating supplementary lighting in combination with the sun protection system, heating, cooling and mechanical ventilation – on a control panel, customised for this building. One of these control panels is mounted next to every office door.

To ensure the appropriate use of natural ventilation through the opening of windows, the occupants can consult the control panel which will indicate on a display when the opening of windows could lead to a loss of comfort or even to operating failures due to external influences (such as low temperatures, high winds...). The following parameters were used as a measure for trouble-free office operation:
· Daily weather forecasts supplied by the Essen weather station;
· The temperature inside the two façade layers (façade corridor) is recorded at various altitudes and in several directions and the data transmitted to the building's central computer;
· Current wind speeds are recorded at rooftop level, translated into data for various altitudes and transmitted to the building's central computer;
· The central computer displays all offices where a window has been opened and transmits this data to the telephone system;
· The cooling ceiling elements automatically stop cooling an office in which a window has been opened;
· The ambient brightness is analysed for the automatic adjustment of the external sun protector blinds.
Furthermore, a user-strategy has been devised, illustrating activities as well as results to be achieved.

The various technical functions such as lighting, ventilation, cooling, fire extinguishing, etc. are integrated in a multi-functional ceiling element that is the result of numerous tests with regards to cooling, ventilation and smoke extraction properties carried out in the ROM laboratories, where different outlet types and configurations were analysed and optimised. The selected type of ceiling element took the form of a technical duct that accommodates ventilation (long vents), lighting (down lights, involute lamps), sprinklers, smoke detectors and loudspeakers. Above the perforated ceiling panels to both sides of the technical duct the convective cooling ceilings have been installed; their maximum output is 125 W/m^2 (16/18°C).

The cooling ceilings are supplied by a ring system in the corridor for a maximum simultaneous cooling rate per floor of 25 kW. The risers in the shaft have been dimensioned for a maximum simultaneity of 0.8. To reduce the shaft surfaces, the climate control unit supplying the offices and inner zones from the 1st to the 27th floor has been installed in the 17th and 18th floors. The generation of the required total volume of air has been delegated to two fans operating in parallel, with an output of 60,830 m^3/h each; the fans are able to equalise variable volume flow and pressure differences of the intake and air extraction vents due to an integrated revolution regulator. To ensure the required values are maintained, the following areas have been divided into zones according to the user profile:
· Zone 01/00 special rooms 1st - 3rd floors, and offices
· Zone 01/01 offices 4th - 22nd floor NE
· Zone 01/02 core zones 1st - 22nd floors
· Zone 01/03 front-of-elevator areas 1st - 27th floors
· Zone 01/04 conference rooms 1st - 22nd floors
The typical floors are equipped with volume maintainers and zone after-heaters for the SW and NE façade.

Central climate control unit on level -3 supplying special underground areas. Compartment-type central air supply and extraced air processing plants for kitchens, conference zones etc. incl. media equipment.

User strategy of individual function zones

	appropriate usage (consulting the control panel)	inappropriate usage (ignoring the control panel)
Offices Air temperatures winter Air temperatures summer general conditions	> 22°C < 27°C · draught-free office air (w ≤ 0.3 m/s) · no condensation on cooling surfaces · acceptable opening forces on interior doors (≤4Kg) · good balance of heating and cooling energy	poss. < 10°C poss. > 32°C · draught effects (w= up to 1 m/s) · no condensation on cooling surfaces · interior doors difficult to open (more than 10Kg) · increased energy consumption for heating and cooling
Corridors general conditions	· draught-free (w ≤ 0.6 m/s) · interior doors easy to open (≤10Kg)	· draught effects · interior doors at times difficult to open (more than 10Kg)
Lobby Air temperatures winter Air temperatures summer general conditions	> 20°C < 27°C · draught-free (w≤0.6 m/s)	poss. < 8°C poss. > 32°C · draught effects

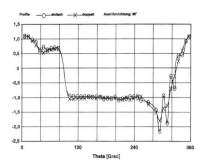

The pressure curve around the entire building shows pronounced lee and windward areas with strong suction peaks, depending on wind speed and wind direction.

The individual climate control main units and building zones are arranged in stacked cooling/heating-supply sub-stations; the stacking order is pressure-related.

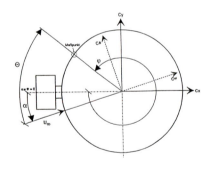

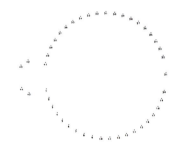

The wind tunnel tests and calculations required the definition of a set of common measurement-points around the entire building.

For the levels -1 to -3, an area of special usage with varying user times, individual control per room is envisaged through after-heaters.

The executive floors (23-26) are equipped with air conditioning that can be adjusted per room and that generates a higher air change. The room zones can be switched off individually, in view of the different user patterns.

The wind tunnel tests revealed a wind pressure dispersion around the tower between windward and lee-side of cp=1.0 - 2.0, so that the configuration and dimensioning of the external air and extracted air vents had to be carefully planned. To prevent wind pressures impeding the system's supply and extracted air flows – while at the same time ensuring that extracted air is swept away from the façade even in high winds so that a build-up of ice on the façade at low temperatures can be avoided – the planners opted for single-jet outlet blowers configured in a semi-circular fashion around the tower. The pressure profile revealed that, due to the cylindrical shape of the building, maximum wind pressure drops rapidly on the windward side; this means that the necessary system pressure to produce the out-let blower speed of 5m/s required for high winds can be dramatically reduced if the configuration of outlet blower vents is completely variable in its orientation. If air is extracted evenly from all nozzles simultaneously, the outlet speed is c. 5m/s at zero wind speed; consequently, in windy conditions the outlet speeds will be smaller/reversed or larger, depending on the location of the vents, due to varying single volume streams. For this reason, individual air extraction vents can be closed via motorised flaps if outlet speeds should necessitate this. This measure, however, leads to varying pressure loss during the extraction process.

The pressure loss in the air chambers during air ingression and extraction at zero wind speed is c. 250 Pa.

The wind pressure exerted on the building ranges from +600 Pa in the pressure zone to -1,100 Pa in the suction zone.

The wind blowing against the vents has a substantial impact on the operation of the fans. The pressure required for extracting air in the air extraction chamber is in this case +731 Pa, but the sub-pressure in the suction chamber is -552 Pa. These adverse conditions will incur a much higher pressure differential of c. 1,380 Pa.

Apart form the average pressure conditions in the chambers outlined above, the volume flow inside the individual vents is also known; it varies greatly due to the pressure conditions on the building's external façade.

To equalise the differences outlined above, ring-shaped suction and air extraction chambers are installed; these are connected to frequency-controlled fans that, in conjunction with the air extraction flaps, ensure trouble-free operation.

The impact of a partly open façade and an extreme windward/lee situation on the supply and extracted air flow per storey represented a further problem area. The aerodynamic simulations revealed a potential danger of adverse impacts, in extreme cases a reversal of air streams inside the air supply ducts, across all floors as well as inside a given floor. To reduce this phenomenon, which a naturally ventilated high-rise building is particularly prone to, volume maintainers and solid resistors were installed in the outlets on each floor.

Additional air supply aggregates for the various user-zones were installed in the main control units on level -3 for the kitchen + auxiliary rooms, restaurant, conference room, lobby, technical installations room and storage rooms, and on the top floor for special functions such as stairwell pressure-ventilation and smoke extraction. External air supply and air extraction are ensured by a floor-level duct with suction and air extraction units in the external system. Shear blowers with adjustable vanes, which ensure constant pressure in the external air supply and air extraction ducts, have been installed to equalise the varying air volumes of the c. 10 climate control-aggregates and the cooling air of the heat rejection aggregates.

Special types of air ducts were used to serve the boardroom on the 27th floor and the lobby zone, taking the specific equipment and user-structures in these areas into account. The glass dome skylight in the boardroom has two functions: to establish visual contact with the outside world and to provide natural daylight. Air conditioning could, therefore, not be directed inside the ceiling; instead, a ventilation system was

Left: Appearance and positioning of the air supply (suction) and air extraction vents inside the double-layer façade of the technical installations floor (17th/18th) supplying the offices throughout the building. The total air volume is c. 120,000 m³/h.

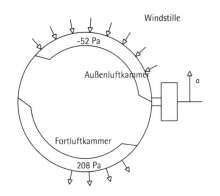
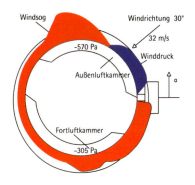

Left: pressure differential between the air supply/extracted air chambers and ambient pressure (nominal volume stream, zero wind speed, 50% of extracted air vents closed);
Right: pressure differential between the air supply/extracted air chambers and ambient pressure (nominal volume stream, 32m/s wind speed, 50% of extracted air vents closed);

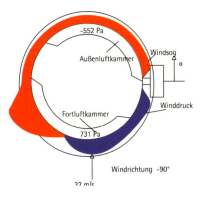
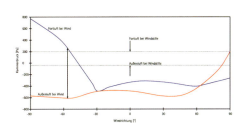

Left: pressure differential between the outside air and extracted air chambers for nominal volume stream at 32m/s wind speed and zero wind speed depending on wind direction

installed inside the cavity floor with a perforated surface. On days with little turbulence, this system supports the natural thermic conditions and also diverts potential pollutants from the room. To select the ideal type of carpet with regards to the required air-permeability, several tests with various carpet types were conducted by the ROM laboratories. To prevent disagreeable radiation through the transparent roof surfaces in summer and winter, a water-filled heating and cooling system running inside the sections has been used that supports the building's main heating and cooling system.

The lobby's large transparent façade surfaces and open-plan access to underground levels provided the planners with a particular challenge in selecting suitable systems for smoke extraction measures and thermic screening measures. The selected air supply system provides a thermic screen in summer and winter via air-filled façade sections. An extraction system located at the cores ensures full smoke extraction in the lobby and the underground levels in conjunction with the relevant façade openings on level -1.

Each stairwell plus access area is equipped with pressure-ventilation to ensure full smoke extraction in case of fire. During normal operation, a 1-fold air change is ensured by blowing fresh air and overflow into each storey. In case of fire the central fire detector unit will cause an increase of air volume to 25,000 m^3/h. The legally required maximum differential pressure in the air-lock of 50 Pa is ensured by an excess-pressure-blind in the stairwell ceiling.

The planners feared that the expected thermic lift forces in the building could cause the mechanical excess-pressure flap to be permanently open during winter and that the smoke extraction through the top of the stairwells could cause substantially more air to enter the ground floor. The planners therefore installed, in agreement with the fire protection officer, smoke detector-activated extraction flaps at the top of the stairwells and fitted the excess-pressure-blind with a light-dome that would be opened in case of fire.

Cooling supply

On level -3, three 700 kW-refrigeration plants cover the building's cold water requirements. The refrigerant used is R134a. The condensation heat of 891 kW each is discharged via evaporation liquefiers. For this purpose, every refrigeration plant is connected to an evaporation liquefier which contains the condensator and a pre-sequenced slat cooler. In the summer the condensator is operated by spraying which is switched off during winter to prevent frost and mist formation. The slat-cooler is principally dry-operated and predominantly serves to enhance performance during winter. Due to reduced liquefying rates during winter the refrigeration plants are turned down to minimal output (140 kW). External and extracted air supply for the evaporation liquefiers is effectuated via the floor-level ducts. The generator-network is separated from the demand point-network by a bypass with two buffer storage units. This allows the refrigeration plants to operate with a constant volume flow, while the demand point network remains variable in accordance with the required refrigeration rate. Switching the refrigeration plants on and off is controlled by a heat volume counter fitted in the main return of the demand point network, in accordance with the required rate.

The main supply for all cold-water demand points is ensured by the central control units with pressure-controlled, redundant supply pumps on levels -3 and 18.

The downstream installations are divided into three pressure zones for the supply of the climate control-aggregates, circulating air-refrigeration plants and cooling ceilings, which are convector-types with a total surface of around 4,000 m^2 and an output of c. 580 kW.

System separation is effectuated by plate-type heat exchangers. Every cooling water network is fitted with a revolution-controlled double pump (main/reserve).

Lighting
Clemens Tropp and Ulrich Werning

Pictures taken at night illustrate clearly the homogenous and continuous lighting concept of the cylindrical building, while particular areas are highlighted with stronger and more brilliant lighting.

In the perception of architecture lighting plays an important role. The character and physical qualities of lighting can, of course, be employed in many different ways. Since the new RWE headquarters rises 162 metres above its urban environment it has a strong impact on the urban landscape of Essen and, consequently, a carefully conceived lighting concept is required. The tower's transparent façade, the main functions of which are to provide the occupants with an unrestricted view as well as a ensuring maximum use of daylight, is a powerful mediator between the building and its environment. As the day progresses, the changing light is reflected in the curved glass, turning the tower into a chameleon-like creature. The reflections on the sheath of glass are like a permanent guise of various lighting moods, from a warm amber glow to a colourless icy sheen.

At night, when the reflective armour is dismantled in the dark, the sharp contours of the giant's interior mechanics become visible. Resembling an étagère with 27 stacked plates, the building opens up, revealing office life to outside observers and creating its own world of light; the building is stunningly illuminated by a plethora of office lights.

The effect is enhanced by a lighting concept that highlights the building's and the garden's characteristic architectural features. The building is not, however, flood-lit. The distinctive structure of the rooftop underlines the lighthouse character of the building and was therefore given a dramatic nocturnal appearance. The rooftop pin is evenly lit right up to its point, cutting through the dark night sky like a burning needle. The circular platform – with its distinctive slat-structure – from which the pin rises, is lit from below, attracting the curiosity of all those people far away who are intrigued by this mysterious, high-tech object. Pin and platform are illuminated by spot lights fitted with halogen vapour lamps; reflector geometry and optical filters have been optimised for this purpose.

At night, the building is illuminated to appear as a homogenous object. Homogeneity and continuity create a sense of calm and order; to achieve this effect, the lighting concept throughout the building had to be based on similar colours of light and lighting principles. However, the separate zones such as casino, lobby, offices, boardroom and rooftop remain distinguishable at night due to their location within the building.

As one approaches the building from the front, the 25-metre high loggia roof gradually appears. The loggia roof, which links the tower to the adjacent buildings, is lit from within the water basin, so that the water movement is projected onto the underside of the loggia roof as well as the front glass façade. The area below the loggia roof is evenly illuminated, without exaggerated accentuation, by narrow-beam, concealed spot lights built into the roof. In the basin, bubble blowers provide an additional play of light. Behind the building, the view expands onto the lake which remains unlit, like a natural lake. The terrace and lake surface are virtually flush. The lake-side edge of the terrace is marked by an underlit seating unit that follows the terrace's undulating contours. This distinctive illuminated separation of terrace and lake is reflected on the lake's surface at night. The illumination of the gardens is very restrained – only a few trees are lit from below – so that the garden's natural character and spaciousness is preserved.

Upon entering the lobby, its transparency is instantly apparent. The direct downlights, which minimise reflections on the glazed vertical surfaces, work in unison with the lobby's transparency. The lobby also features the radially arranged technical ducts in the ceiling that the office floors are equipped with, only in the lobby they are fitted with HIT-70 watt downlights. All HIT lights are fitted with ceramic burners which provide identical and consistent colours and therefore contribute to the homogeneity of the entire lighting concept.

The load-bearing structure of the vaulted architectural concrete ceiling from the supports to the centrepoint is highlighted by a special lighting concept. A canvass is suspended across each of the non-load-bearing cavities of the ceiling vault, leaving a gap around the canvass perimeter. Lights are installed in the space between canvass and ceiling, so the light they produce shines through the gap and onto the white concrete of the load-bearing ceiling parts, highlighting their unusual shape. The canvass itself remains dark in order to produce the necessary contrast. The lights are placed at small, regular intervals and feature a specially formed reflector. The direction and brightness of each spotlight has been manually adjusted. The entire orchestra of spot-lights, hidden from view behind the canvasses, provide a homogenous and harmonious lighting effect.

The office lighting concept, with a day and a night setting, provides maximum comfort. The settings can be activated by the occupants. At night illumination is

Thanks to the sun protector blinds and anti-glare screens fitted to the glass façade the influx of daylight and time settings for artificial lighting can be regulated.

provided with downlights producing a warm white light. In order to minimise any vertical dazzle, i.e. when looking straight into the lights from below, the lights have been fitted with special diffusers. Special reflectors in the light minimise direct glare.

Involute lamps, producing a neutral white light, are employed to complement natural daylight. Involute lamp technology helps to minimise reflective glare. All lighting systems are integrated flush into the technical duct in the ceiling which also accommodates sprinklers, loudspeakers, etc.

The boardroom is fitted with built-in downlights equipped with halogen lamps. The central skylight allows a vertical view up towards the illuminated rooftop platform. The casino is fitted with narrow-beam built-in halogen downlights with minimum glare effect. The halogen lamps provide a brilliant light with excellent colour reproduction, which is particularly important in the dining area.

The dramatic lighting concept highlights the three-dimensional aspect of the ground floor ceiling.

Models
Till Briegleb,
Christoph Ingenhoven
and Klaus Frankenheim

Above: Competition model Commerzbank AG, Frankfurt (6/91)
Left: Competition model RWE AG, Essen (6/91)

In the development of an exemplary product it is the experiment that reigns supreme. With every stage, new complexities and conditions need to be evaluated. Erroneous decisions can cause fatal chain-reactions particularly in architecture, where a web of artistic, practical, scientific and technical considerations may – even in projects with clearly defined goals – cause confusion in the solution-finding process. In order to overcome this potential problem, it is paramount to examine and evaluate relevant data throughout the entire design process with the help of models. Hence, experiments on models in various scales representing small-scale or part versions of real-life conditions stood at the centre of the planning process for the RWE tower.

The fact that a completely new type of high-rise architecture – an architecture almost without precedent, a prototype even – was predominantly developed with three-dimensional models and not – as most contemporary projects are – with CAD, may initially seem curious. But the fact remains that our imagination and perception is more at home in a tactile and tangible world – despite the ever-increasing virtuality of our lives. Although this form of planning – the concrete validation of planning ideas through the making of models – leads to an increased workload, it remains the only valid approach towards a solution that is successful in all given aspects.

The planning for the RWE tower began in 1991, when Ingenhoven Overdiek und Partner were working on two competitions simultaneously: the urban planning competition for RWE/Ruhrkohle in Essen and the competition for the Commerzbank tower in Frankfurt, where Christoph Ingenhoven was awarded the second prize after Lord Norman Foster's winning entry.

After Christoph Ingenhoven was commissioned with the building of the new RWE headquarters he was able to adapt the findings from the Frankfurt competition – in which the engineer Frei Otto had co-operated with

This 1:200 model (autumn 1993) still features the helipad on the top of the building (above) and initial ideas for the re-design of the Opernplatz between RWE site and Aalto theatre.

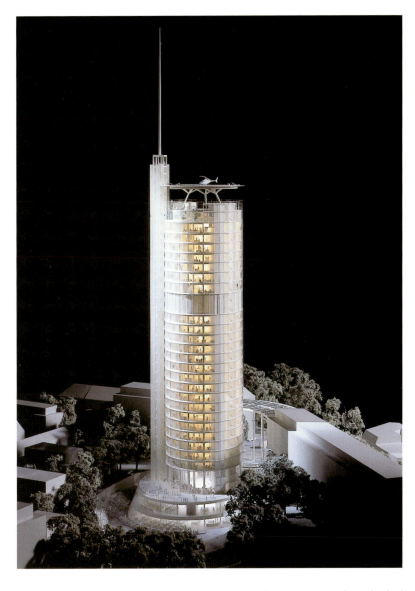

The 1:200 model was used to examine the effect of the building on its surroundings at night time.

This model shows the accentuated lighting concept for the special basement zones, lobby and forecourt; the model featured extremely detailed lighting in order to provide as realistic an impression as possible of the desired highlighting effect.

Christoph Ingenhoven – in a productive manner. An adaptation was necessary because the brief in Essen demanded a much smaller building than the one in Frankfurt. Nevertheless, several elements, such as the ideal basic shape – in energetics terms – of a circular column as well as the double-layer glass façade, did not need to be conceived from scratch. The 'fault list' for problem zones in conventional high-rises – which had formed part of the Commerzbank planning process and included issues like permanently locked windows, inappropriate interior climate and sun protection, dark internal areas, poor internal communication, high energy consumption – could now be meticulously analysed and adapted for the RWE tower.

Following the submission of the development plan and the preliminary plans for building, façade, load-bearing structure and technical concepts during the course of 1992, the stage of intensive studies with models began in 1993. To begin with, a 1:200 model was built to examine the urban context as well as the composition of building blocks and open spaces.

Aerophysical macro and micro tests conducted at the Aachen Institut für Industrieaerodynamik (IFI) were used to calculate and analyse the macro and micro biological impact of the intended building development. At that stage, the arrangement and size of the loggia roof and the provision of recreational areas on the terraces were determined. On November 22, 1993, RWE successfully demanded 21 modifications to be made to the final plans that formed part of the final planning application; the general design of the building was now agreed and the complex development of the high-rise building concept involving numerous 1:200 to 1:1 models began in earnest. Models are used to such a large extent in the planning process of the RWE project – which, by the way, did not render the drawing of almost 6,000 plans superfluous – beacause they highlight detailed problem areas much more clearly than plans and force the planners to find a solution, usually by way of making another model. Taking this course of action is surely justified considering that this endeavour is largely informed by a desire to eliminate past sins in high-rise construction.

Before final assembly, the architects reviewed each model with Amalgam Modelmakers, who then gave the go-ahead for all parts and components of each individual model to be assembled.

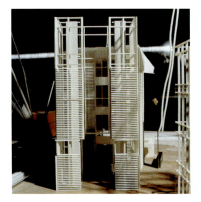

The selection of colours, materials and surface quality of the final model was based on studies with detailed part-models.

The top of the building at shell stage, before the installation of the façade.

The photographic documentation of the model covering all intermediate construction phases clearly illustrates the way in which the building would later be constructed: a number of separate pre-fabricated elements and components that are assembled on site.

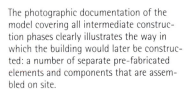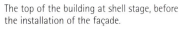

The two pictures on the right show the lighting details in the 1:50 models: the light travels from a central source through several fibre glass cables to their respective light emitting end points. In order to enable the electrification of the entire model, the cables running along the reflective ceiling plan (far right) were fixed to central 'risers' inside the shafts with soldered connectors.

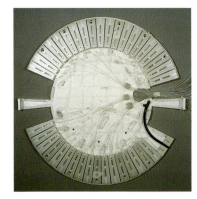

Alongside various models of building details made by the architects themselves, planning development evolved largely around two large models: a 1:1 façade model made by façade specialists Gartner and several 1:50 models made by Amalgam modelmakers, Bristol, UK.

From autumn 1994 until summer 1995 Amalgam built a three-part model of the entire building. The bottom part comprised the foundation, lobby and first floor; the middle part included the technical installations floor with one floor below and above; the third part consisted of the executive floors at the top, the roof and rooftop installations. All parts could be opened to reveal the interior. The modelmakers, led by Sandy Copeman, created a model with astonishing detail – 2,500 tiny people populated the miniature tower with its precisely reproduced lighting fixtures and furniture. With a model of this calibre at their disposal, the Ingenhoven Overdiek und Partner team was able to develop and examine their design ideas in great detail.

This way of working would normally require the architects to produce highly detailed plans which they were not able to provide at that stage of the design process, causing a certain amount of friction and incurring increased costs. The 'eccentric modelmakers' (Ingenhoven) aired their frustration caused by the architects' never-ending last-minute modifications by inundating Ingenhoven Overdiek und Partner with humorous faxes; they also eventually demanded higher fees to prevent going bankrupt. In the end, the architects themselves paid the difference as the benefits of such a detailed model had proved invaluable. The level of perfection achieved in the making of the model caused the German architects to become frequent flyers: they spent around £18,000 on flights between Düsseldorf and England alone.

During the completion of the construction process, the architects experienced a few surprising déjà-vus, no doubt thanks to the detailed, highly accurate and realistic models. The formidable precision and detail in the planning process and the homogenous, elegant appearance of the finished building could arguably not have been achieved so successfully were it not for the – by today's CAD-standards almost antiquated – process of modelmaking. Several years of research with glass façade models also contributed substantially to the successful application of the ambitious design ideas. Over a period of one and a half years the architects and façade specialists Gartner simulated high-rise reality at an altitude of 25 metres with a 1:1 model, under the

Elevation of the lobby area, 1:50 model

In a computer simulation the three separate 1:50 part-models were merged into one virtual glass model which already had a strong resemblance to the finished building that was about to be erected.

The Amalgam Modelmakers' workshop in Bristol, UK

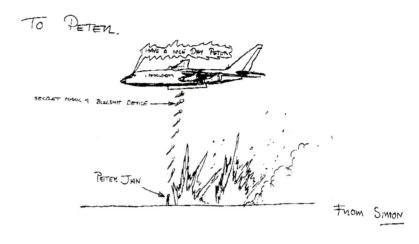

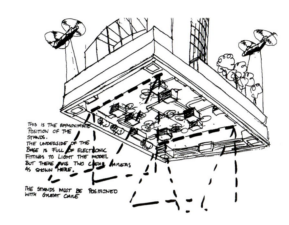

Above: Amalgam Bristol sends 3-D-instructions on how to install and exhibit the model. During the various modelmaking phases, architects and modelmakers discussed details and final plans per phone and fax on a daily basis. Surprisingly, both teams had time to draw a few humorous sketches in between all those technical drawings, and these sketches show how German and English humour can work together perfectly.

The models were constructed in a way that allowed interior photographs to be made. The photos show the precision of the models' surfaces and details. The detailed models were particularly effective in the development of the reflective ceiling plans and the lighting concept, devised in co-operation with lighting experts Ulrich Werning and Clemens Tropp.

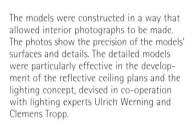

auspices of Gartner's energetic director Dr. Fritz Gartner, who never tired of refuting the many voices of scepticism as to the impossibility of such a façade with a dry 'Don't worry, it'll work'. The model comprised one façade element with a sealed 'office' behind it. The office was crammed with measuring devices, providing relatively precise data as to potential energy savings and the period of time throughout a year that the wind pressures allow a window to be opened.

The large number of façade elements – 1,000 – that were eventually manufactured for swift and trouble-free installation clearly justified the elaborate prototyping stage. 1:1 models were also successfully used for testing all the other façade types in this project, notably the elevator tower and the hydraulic gate in the restaurant.

The large-scale, structurally imperative planning processes alone put considerable pressure on the planning schedule and logistics; the architects' meticulous attention to detail in putting their design concept into practice intensified the pressure even further. Christoph Ingenhoven says that '... our planning stretched far beyond handing over the keys'. The architects worked on more than 20 special planning permissions and one building permission that the City of Essen building authority had gran-ted in conjunction with several expert departments of the regional authorities – not by the letter but in the spirit of high-rise building regulations – so that the unusual concept could be realised. Of course, the architects also had to deal daily with unforeseen problems in their attempt to execute their work to the highest standards. Christoph Ingenhoven and his team scrutinised the grouting of the tiling in the sanitary zones with the same zeal as the construction of the natural stone waterfalls.

Christoph Ingenhoven confirms the 'total love and devotion in planning and execution' that his team displayed throughout the project. The occupants and visitors of the RWE tower are privileged to experience the fruit of this labour on a daily basis.

Full-size façade mock-ups and detail models of, for example, air locks, stairwells and elevator lobbies were of the highest precision so that they could be used as the basis for major future design decisions.

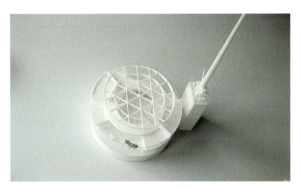
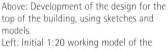

Above: Development of the design for the top of the building, using sketches and models.
Left: Initial 1:20 working model of the panoramic elevators in the lobby.

Garden
Till Briegleb,
Christoph Ingenhoven
and Klaus Klein

Spiral fog

The transparent, horizontally structured glass column of the RWE tower easily conjures up associations with an oceanic tornado, a 'hydro twister' right there in the middle of Germany. The inherent energy of enormous rotational forces appears to be almost tangible even from far away, and seems to increase the closer one gets. Standing before the building, this metaphor becomes fact. The garden behind the tower absorbs the rotational energy of the tower and brings a calmness to the scene. A lake, the paths, the walls and plants draw the lines of currents, representing a huge spinning motion. No matter which perspective you choose, either from the building via an ebbing sense of movement that ends in the stillness of the gardens or from the end of the garden up towards the magnetic force of the glass tower, both perspectives perfectly describe the alliance of an architectural and a landscaping concept.

Instead of reducing the gardens to pure decorative feature or colourful fringe for an object with a very strong presence, Christoph Ingenhoven and the landscape architects Klaus Klein and Rolf Maas of Weber Klein Maas have aimed to blend nature and technology without denying their fundamentally contrasting appearance. Even in the extremely staged manner of this garden, the contrast between vegetation and construction, change and longevity, flux and stability remains perceptible. However, the powerful ties connecting the building with the gardens convey how much technology owes to the abstraction of nature; imaginative minds are now bringing this heritage back to life.

The initial winning urban planning concept submitted for the competition – at that stage the brief covered the entire former Stern Brewery site – already envisaged the notion of a garden, and this notion never lost its signifi-

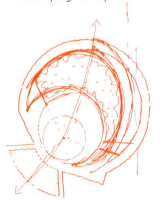

This sketch shows how the building is linked to the park by the forecourt, the lobby and the terrace.

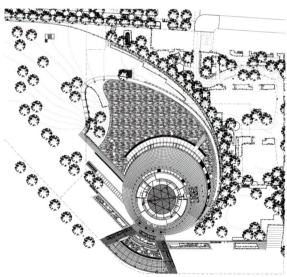

M (1:2,200)

cance throughout the development of the overall concept. The design proposal by Christoph Ingenhoven was the only one that planned to accommodate both RWE's and Ruhrkohle's headquarters in office towers so that the surrounding area would remain free of buildings. The powerful presence of vertically stacked office floors, as embodied by the glass office tower, forms an integral part of the original conception for this project.

Consequently, the initial concept included a garden project for the entire site which became obsolete following the subsequent division of the site into several zones. The same applies to the initial urban planning concept with which Christoph Ingenhoven won the competition; their concept could also only be partially realised as the two clients, RWE and Ruhrkohle, pursued different interests. For the planning of green spaces around adjacent residential properties the architects were reduced to a not particularly influential advisor position. On the other hand, the architects were granted free range to design the RWE garden in co-operation with the landscape architects. In this garden, different conceptual layers merge to form a homogenous unit.

The result is the graphic concept of the powerful spiral and the overall colour concept – referred to by office staff as 'alpine' and continued in the building's interior – an ambiance concept that borrows from Japanese garden design, focussing on the art of contemplation and on the power of contrast.

The graphic concept outlined before comprises five components: a gently curved path leading from the circular platform of the entrance area down into the garden below; a wall along the path that screens the adjacent residential properties from the site and that symbolises the difference in height of almost 6 metres

The former Stern Brewery shortly before demolition

The excavation site of the natural stone used in the RWE project, at the Splügenpass, near the Swiss-Italian border.

Inspirational picture of the Temple District in Kyoto, Japan.

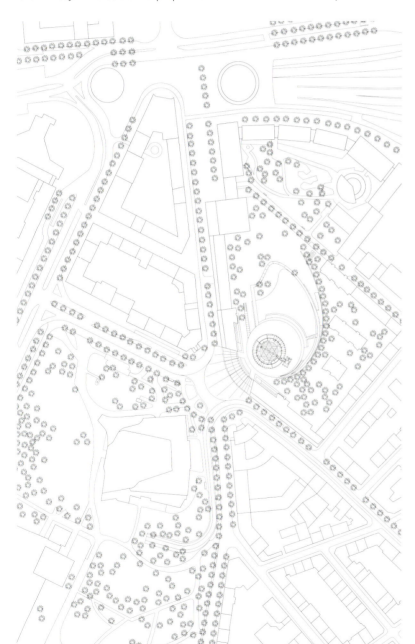

The site plan (M 1:3,500) shows how the park of the 'Stern' service industry area is inte-grated into the City of Essen's existing green link.

View of the parks and gardens with blossoming rhododendron bushes

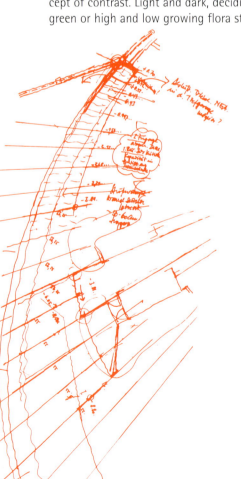

Christoph Ingenhoven's sketches clearly illustrate the close geometrical link between basement façade, waterfalls and circular path.

between entrance and garden levels; the planting of maple trees, rhododendron bushes and pear trees by the wall; the elegant shape of the lake that forms the centre of the park and for the design of which no less than 17 radii had to be combined, and finally the green space at the end of the site with many trees, describing the smooth transition of movement spilling out into a wide open space.

The 'alpine' colour concept, which Christoph Ingenhoven also calls 'reduced photosynthesis', determines the selection of plants and materials. The tower's elegance was not to be spoiled by an array of colourful floral patterns. Reduction and clear lines to underline the appearance of the building were the order of the day, and the restrained alpine colours were obviously more suitable than the bold and loud colour scheme of a Dutch tulip field. The intentional emphasis on green and white blossoms as well as the colour explosion of an Indian Summer were the main criteria in the search for suitable vegetation. The selection finally included rhododendron, pear trees, water lilies and azaleas, all with white blossoms, and as a subtle variation a maple tree whose blossoms are a delicate yellow. An avenue of marsh oaks on the garden border along with the maple and pear tree make for a perfectly golden Indian Summer when their leaves glow in an autumnal colour palette of red, orange and yellow.

Other plants were used to further emphasise the concept of contrast. Light and dark, deciduous and evergreen or high and low growing flora strike a balance that would be difficult to achieve without this dialogue. Alongside the rhododendron, cherry bay leaf shrubs planted along the wall provide dark evergreen spots of colour and underline the variable height of the terrain. Rhododendron bushes, pear and maple trail the wall, thus maintaining the wall's graphic contours when the maple sheds its leaves in the winter.

The green colour of the lawn also plays a major part in this colour composition, while at the same time providing an uncluttered, contemplative space within the otherwise rather confined terrain. Speckled with numerous small flower beds, the lawn forms an extension of the lake's surface, creating a sense of reduced serenity so typical for Japanese temple gardens, especially when viewed from the terrace and the canteen.

The 120-metre cyclopean wall is made from layers of the regional stone, Ruhr sandstone, procured during the site excavation, thus serving as a geological reminder of the brute force of the excavation. The strong colours of the stone wall – an earthy blend of yellow, red, brown and black – stand in stark contrast to the building, creating yet another element of electric tension between the glass tower and its setting. Rustic/high-tech, old/young, rough/smooth – the poetic contradictions are conveyed without drama. The alpine theme is picked up once more by the heaped stone base of the path leading down to the lake, conjuring up images of landslides or avalanche slopes.

In conjunction with the azaleas on the hill on the opposite side – physically denoting the difference in altitude between the site and the adjacent plot – the

Apart from aluminium, glass and the polished natural stone Verde Spluga used for the building, a local sandstone found on site was used as lake-side gravel and in the construction of a wall in the RWE gardens.

Top: Rhododendron 'Cunningham's White' (Azalea 'Palestrina'), White water-lily (Nymphaea Albida), White azalea (Azalea 'Mount Everest'), Cornelian Cherry (Cornus Mas)
Bottom: Cornelian Cherry (Cornus Mas), Japanischer Ahorn (Acer Palmatum), Amelanchier Lamarckii, Pin Oak (Quercus Palustris)

cyclopean wall creates a perfect isolation from the rather banal aesthetics of the area surrounding the site that would otherwise disrupt the contemplative aspect of the gardens.

The bamboo planted around the water islets in the light wells brings the Far-Eastern element of self-awareness to these gardens, a theme that is continued in the rooftop vegetation. The architects placed bamboo walls in the rooftop garden and in front of the windows on the executive floors, creating an alpine atmosphere, particularly on a foggy or cloudy day.

The landscape concept further includes: the outside extension of the canteen by way of a terrace; the entire water course, beginning with basins and fountains in the building's courtyard, continuing via two light wells

Due to the transparency of the glazed basement façade the parks and gardens outside become part of the interior landscape.

Left: the inspiration for the natural stone wall
Right: a detail of the erected natural stone wall built with the regional sandstone found on site during excavation and demolition

to the left and right of the building, into the water falls cascading into the lake with its bed lined in black; and, finally, the planned art piece by Robert Long, made of Neanderthal chalk stone and 32 metres long, picking up the tower's diameter.

Another aspect of great importance is the urban context of the site, as the replacement of the former Stern Brewery with the RWE development has created a completely new situation at the Opernplatz, the piazza in front of Alvar Aalto's opera house, which required the architects extend their planning scope beyond the RWE site. Furthermore, the creation of the RWE headquarters on this particular site created the unique opportunity to vastly improve the unattractive area around the railway station by linking the northern and southern halves of downtown Essen, hitherto separated by the railway tracks.

Finding a logical solution to link the popular shopping area north of the central train station with the service sector zone, dominated by large corporate headquarters, to the south of the station, was one of the fundamental ideas behind the Passarea Project devised by Ingenhoven Overdiek und Partner. This concept, with a completely new central station at its core, opens the barriers to provide a new link between the shopping and office quarters. In order to arrive at a sensible solution for this link, however, the urban planning aspects of the northern area needed to be fundamentally improved. For this purpose, Ingenhoven Overdiek und Partner was convinced that between the opera, public park, Hochtief

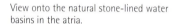

View onto the natural stone-lined water basins in the atria.

Left: Bamboo (Phyllostachis Glauca)
Right: view from the garden level central lobby to the conference zone's central patio

View onto the central patio which provides daylight for the conference zone lobby and the conference rooms. The bamboo serves to diffuse the light and screen the conference rooms from direct visibility.

View into the restaurants' atria

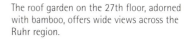

The roof garden on the 27th floor, adorned with bamboo, offers wide views across the Ruhr region.

HQ and RWE HQ the Opernplatz would have to lose its characteristics of a muddled traffic intersection. The orientation of the opera building – which Aalto wisely turned away from the unattractive urban mess and towards the city park – can only be correctly incorporated into the Passarea concept if the green zone of trees around the opera building is extended all the way to the RWE tower and if bus routes, tram lines and car traffic are diverted to create a new pedestrian link to the railway station. This would transform the Opernplatz once more into a thriving, vibrant and exciting piazza and at the same time provide a point of departure for the future revitalisation of the northern city centre.

Project History
Achim Nagel and
Lars Leitner

Competition

Early 1991
RWE AG and Ruhrkohle AG (RAG) decide to jointly hold a competition with an urban-planning content for the site of the former Stern brewery and the site of the Ruhrkohle AG headquarters south of Essen central station. The competition brief calls for the planning of a 'new centre for the service sector with administrative buildings, shops, apartments, a hotel and leisure facilities such as restaurants. The two competition organisers are to be the premier occupants of the new office spaces.

Spring 1991
Competition documents are dispatched.

20 June, 1991
The prize jury, chaired by Peter Zlonicky, awards the first prize (DM 75,000) to the partnership Ingenhoven/Bob Gansfort, Düsseldorf. The second and third prizes are awarded to Hentrich, Petschnigg & Partner, Düsseldorf and Auer & Weber, Munich, respectively.

The prize jury's comments on the winning entry are as follows: 'The winning entry provides a particularly suitable framework for the further development and qualification of the planned construction. The authors of the winning entry are to be commissioned with the development of their proposal and with the planning of the RWE site in the spirit of the competition. The development concept for the site's central area requires the creation of distinctive boundaries between built-up zones and areas that are to remain free of buildings; the concept also needs to provide a convincing urban landscape solution with large recreational areas. For the redesign of the RAG complex, a suitable qualification process involving several participants in the competition should be instigated. Alternatively, the integration of the existing RAG building should be investigated.'

In 1991 and 1992 the following parameters were set for the continuation of the project:
· RAG decide to continue their project independently.
· The planning for all peripheral buildings, incl. underground parking, is to be executed by the 2nd prize winner, HPP Hentrich- Petschnigg & Partners.
· The architect Bob Gansfort is commissioned to build the residential buildings, incl. underground parking, and the high-rise building on Rellinghauser Straße.
· As the guiding force behind the working group of participating architects, Christoph Ingenhoven Architects and Engineers are commissioned with the realisation of the project's urban-planning brief, the building of the new RWE headquarters and the creation of a landscape concept.

Planning

1992
In the course of 1992, a development plan, based on the urban-planning concept of the winning entry and preliminary planning of individual parts of the project, is established in co-operation with the City of Essen.

This phase of intensive urban-planning discussion about the part of town adjacent to the station includes the development of urban-planning ideas that would form the basis for the Passarea project planning process in 1993. The concept envisages a vastly improved link between the two hitherto separated city-centre areas north and south of the station. A new railway station and several new office buildings represent the core of the planning concept.

August 1992
The contracts with the architects are signed.

Autumn 1992
Completion of the development plan.

October 1992
Presentation of the preliminary planning documents for the RWE tower to the RWE board. The board charge the architects with further planning of façade, load-bearing structure, technical, urban-planning and general building concepts.

April 1993
Presentation of the double-layer ventilation façade in the form of an integrated study developed by experts.

From June 1993
Aerodynamic macro-tests, conducted by IFI, to calculate wind currents and wind noises affecting the façade.

From August 1993
Aerodynamic micro tests by IFI with the aim of fine-tuning the effects of wind currents and wind noises on the façade.

Early August 1993
Submission of the design plans.

20 August, 1993
Presentation of the design plans to the RWE board.

Early September 1993
Completion of planning permission documents.

The site of the former Stern Brewery shortly before and after demolition

Above: The site around Christmas 1994. The lobby supports and the external cores have already been erected.
Left: Aerial photograph of the recently completed RWE tower, Christmas 1996

September / November 1993
Value engineering process, incl. examination of cost-reduction potential.

22 November, 1993
After comprehensive examinations conducted by RWE, all parties involved in the planning process and experts from Hochtief and Lahmeyer AG, the RWE board draws up a 21-point modification list for the future headquarters building. This list includes cost-reduction measures such as withdrawing the idea of a rooftop helipad, a reduced interior schedule and a reduction in the standards for technical equipment and interior fit-out. The architects are surely dismayed to see the interior staircases discarded, as they had been included to improve communication and spatial qualities. The improvement in surface efficiency requested by the client also results in a tighter axial division. This reduction in tier height permits the addition of two further levels. Hochtief is charged with erecting the building on the basis of the previous planning process and the 21-point list. The architects are appointed executive planners, which includes construction and detail planning, and are asked to conduct the artistic supervision of the project.

19 December, 1993
Submission of modified planning application.

31 March, 1994
Completion of the planning application.

Early April 1994
Delivery of initial executive plans as the basis for the slot and break-through plans and reinforcement schedule. Initial pouring of structural concrete is thus ensured to go ahead in July 1994.

Execution

Early 1993
Commissioning of waste disposal and site excavation.

The excavation of the site to 13 metres below surface level reveals the close-to-surface coal seams Finefrau, Geitling 1 and 2, Kreffenscher 2 and Mausegatt, with thicknesses of up to 1 metre. The loose and moist soil found in two cavities in the Geitling 1 seam is excavated and the cavities filled with lean concrete. Furthermore, the soil of the dried bed of the River Berne, which is filled with aeolian deposits, is replaced to a depth of 3 metres.

Due to the presence of 2nd world war bombs on site all excavated matter was carefully sifted in accordance with the relevant authorities and then taken to be recycled.

Nevertheless, in late 1993 a TNT charge that had taken on the colour of the soil exploded, injuring two workers. Fortunately, this was the only serious incident of its kind during the remaining construction process. The rock stone is quarried with particular care. The site of the RWE tower is in part made up of sandstone rock.

During the site's excavations several coal seams were unearthed, so to speak, that were later filled with concrete. Although the rock had to be excavated with immense effort, it provided ideal conditions for the RWE tower's foundation.

The quarried rock is sorted on-site and then temporarily stored for later re-use. During the landscape planning process it later emerges that the quarried rock could be used in its natural colouring for the undulating cyclopean wall in the park and for the pond banks.

Early 1994
Beginning of the detailed excavations for the preparation of the tower foundation. As the foundation needs to be brought down to a level where carbon layers are present, precautionary methane gas measurements are executed in areas of exposed carbon.

Following the excavation and waste disposal measures, the future site traffic poses a substantial challenge to planners, site management, energy companies and other City of Essen utilities providers, not least because of the work being carried out simultaneously on the adjacent Ruhrkohle site.

Traffic needs to be routed around the site. At the same time, the scheduled service of the tram line running along Gutenberg Straße needs to be maintained. During the excavation phase the streets need to be cleaned daily due to the increased soiling by the delivery lorries. In order to lead pedestrian traffic safely along the site boundaries, pedestrian tunnels need to be constructed and existing footpaths need to be altered.

The construction process on the 17,000 m² site in the city centre requires extensive logistics efforts even before building can begin. An appointment schedule that all contractors are asked to adhere to strictly is set up to regulate delivery and transport of materials; later on, deliveries to the growing building are charged onto two external heavy goods elevators. Logistical optimisation furthermore requires that the tower's core be erected before the peripheral buildings and the underground parking are built.

June 1994
Hochtief apply the base course for the foundation.

July 1994
Shuttering and reinforcement for the tower's foundation plate are completed after five weeks and pass final inspection by the examining structural engineer.

22 July, 1994
The concrete for the foundation plate is poured in one day in order to achieve a monolithic foundation. Due to the high hydration heat, four pumping stations, supplying rubber tubes with cooling water gushing through them, are required for the cooling process. The binding process lasts three weeks and is constantly monitored via temperature sensors integrated in the concrete.

12 September, 1994
Annette Jaeger, mayor of Essen, Dr. Friedhelm Gieske, chairman of RWE and Dr. Hans-Peter Keitel, chairman of Hochtief, lay the foundation stone. The residents around the site listen to the speech at their open windows, noting with joy that they will cordially be invited to the topping-out ceremony.

December 1994
Five months after the first structural concrete has been poured the ground floor concrete ceiling is completed. The 5x6 metre large and 1.5 metre high shuttering made of fibreglass-reinforced plastic for the unusual ceiling shape (internal office speak: 'Porsche wheel') was made by the Seeger company from Stutensee/Hunsrück, who specialise in the manufacture of domed mouldings for the car industry and ship building. After the ceiling's shape and volume has been developed with the aid of three-dimensional calculations and dimensioning systems,

Under the supervision of the architects the fibreglass reinforced shuttering 'pods' for the lobby walls and ceilings were produced in several layers and the surface was carefully perfected. Finally, they were hoisted into place with a special crane and the reinforcement was inserted.

After the site had been cleared of all waste the shuttering and reinforcement for the RWE tower's 3-metre-thick concrete foundation plate were installed. This picture shows the shuttering and foundations of the main cranes that would be stacked as the construction process continued.

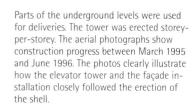

Parts of the underground levels were used for deliveries. The tower was erected storey-per-storey. The aerial photographs show construction progress between March 1995 and June 1996. The photos clearly illustrate how the elevator tower and the façade installation closely followed the erection of the shell.

1:50- and 1:10-scale patterns further optimise the ceiling into its precise and final shape. After the mouldings arrive by special night transport the site team place the reinforcement into the domed moulding. Due to the enormous shuttering pressure, the entire moulding construction needs to be supported right down to foundation level.

All load-bearing reinforced concrete supports and ceilings at garden level and on the ground floor are finished in architectural concrete. Because of the severe winter weather and the extraordinarily complex concreting process of these load-bearing parts made of high-strength concrete, the specialist company Strohmann applies the final finish to the architectural concrete surface once the shell has been completed.

The stone that was to be used in the RWE tower was a natural green stone that Christoph Ingenhoven had discovered in Switzerland. It later emerged that the stone the Swiss referred to as 'Verde Spleer' was also quarried in Italy, where it was known as 'Verde Spluga'. Because natural stone is only quarried during the summer, the stone needed to be selected and quarrying to begin in early 1995. It was quarried in large blocks near the Tessino town Andossi Scrae and then cut to a smaller size in Mönchengladbach by Cancian, who also cut the stone to thickness with diamond saws. The stone pieces were then cut into 8,400 different shapes, the surface flamed for exterior use, polished for interior use and finally numbered piece by piece and brought to the site for fitting.

Februar/March 1995
The next two floors are built on top of the ground floor as brow frameworks with non-changeable static concrete walls.

The erection of the remaining storeys is further optimised by dividing them into two halves and then erecting them step-by-step, thus minimising the number of required pre-fab ceiling shuttering panels that can now be lifted much faster by the crane. Eventually, the completion per half-storey only takes four days. The rationalised building process is continued up to the ceiling above the 17th floor.

October 1995
The two levels housing the building's technical installations, the 18th and 19th floors, prove to be very difficult in terms of construction and building schedule, because the elaborate technical installations only permit very low brow and main beam heights.

While the staircase-cores continue to climb in the conventional manner, the remaining vertical building parts are erected in a single process. Because the building's technical installations are packed very tightly, the five supports on the internal ring need to be replaced. This results in a beam construction that is 1.25 metres thick. It was made with pre-fabricated shuttering cases that in turn were placed onto a continual shuttering. For the external ring with its standard ceiling thickness of 25 centimetres, ceiling shuttering panels from the typical floors can be used.

May 1996
With the completion of the ceiling above the 29th floor the shell is completed on schedule.

After final technical and design points have been resolved with the aid of several sample façades, the mounting of the façade begins. The erection of the shell is carried out six floors in advance of the mounting of the façade. For every section, the next floor up is transformed into the mounting platform. The façade elements are carried to the point of installation by a crab on monorail.

Installation is speedy as the delivered pre-fab façade elements, complete with sun screens, can be fixed to special consoles integrated into the shell, where they are also adjusted for perfect fit. This way, weather permitting, around 50 façade elements can be fitted in one week, the equivalent of almost an entire floor.

The 600 m² sloped façade facing the garden at basement level is a particular challenge for the architects and façade specialists. The geometry of a frustum disc applied here creates a different format for every single window pane.

27 June, 1996
Topping-out-ceremony
Hochtief chairman Dr. Klaus-Peter Keitel announces the completion date of December 31, 1996. RWE chairman Dr. Dietmar Kuhnt declares that the new tower symbolises the reinvention of RWE.

Top row: The natural stone quarry on the Splügenpass in Italy, near the source of the Rhine.
2nd row from top: The mined sand-stone blocks await transportation to Mönchengladbach for cutting.
3rd row from top: The patterns are transfered onto the raw slabs; trial lay-out and numbering of individual slabs.
Above: The raw slabs after being cut to size; the cut-to-size slabs are mounted on site (waterfall, lobby).

In a one-day concreting process the 3-metre strong foundation plate was poured on July 22, 1994. The photos are testimony to the formidable logistic effort on the part of the concrete specialists. At the beginning of the concreting process, several concreting specialists, equipped with special vibrators, had to position themselves between lower and upper reinforcement layer, in order to ensure the proper compression of the concrete.

After the fibre glass/plastic shuttering has been mounted onto a scaffolding above the ground floor, the reinforcement was inserted into the main beams and the vaulted, up to 2-metre thick ceiling compartments. The two photos below show the lobby shortly before the 'Porsche wheel' ceiling – which lends the lobby its distinctive character – was concreted.

21 September, 1996
The aerial and the previously assembled steel platform are installed on the roof with a crane. The interior of the three-part aerial is accessible for assembly and maintenance.

The loggia roof is installed. The loggia roof structure is delivered in several parts and assembled at a nearby coal pit before being lifted on site by three cranes and then secured; the link between the tower and the peripheral buildings, an important urban-planning requirement, is thus established.

The photovoltaic slats are installed on the loggia roof; they produce 19 kWp of electricity which is supplied to the building's internal grid. Excess electricity will be fed to the city's electricity works via a change-over switch.

Autumn 1996
The loggia roof is installed. ....
Next, the photovoltaic slats are istalled on the loggia roof. ....

October 1996
The 11,000 m² façade with its 5,526 window panes is in place.

As the façade is fitted, the pre-installation of the building's technical installations is under way. The wiring is fed along transversal ducts suspended from the ceiling elements by two hooks without disrupting the building process. The final installation is done six months hence. The purpose-built technical duct proves extremely efficient. After the technical equipment is fully installed it takes another few months before the perforated metal side panels can be clipped into place, just before the offices are finished.

November 1996
Initial visits and inspections of individual floors by the future occupant, the RWE.

Up to December 1996
Installation of the building's central computer. Due to the complicated technical adjustments that had to be made once the central computer was installed, the subsequent installation of the elevators threatened to fall seriously behind schedule. The colleagues from Thyssen, however, worked three shifts running round the clock and saved the day.

30 December, 1996
Official completion and final inspection of the building and the exterior grounds.

Early 1997
Final inspection of the remaining interior fit-outs and initial set-up of technical installations and EDP-equipment.

13 March, 1997
Opening celebrations in the presence of the Mayor of Essen, Mrs. Annette Jäger, Dr. Dietmar Kuhnt, chairman of the RWE board and Dr. Wolfhard Leidnitz, Hochtief board member.

10 March, 1998
Almost one year after RWE had moved into their new headquarters, Greenpeace activists occupied the loggia roof in front of the building.

With this direct action, Greenpeace protested against the transit by rail of nuclear waste to the Castor nuclear reprocessing plant near Hanover that caused a storm of protest among parts of the German population at the time; some of the nuclear waste on those trains came from nuclear power stations operated by RWE.

After initial confusion about this spectacular direct action, RWE staff reacted in the spirit of the company's new and open identity, as symbolised by the new RWE building, and invited the Greenpeace activists to discuss the matter over tea and biscuits.

Manufacture of the Thyssen elevators, from sample cabins to the completed elevator system.

Shortly before the completion of the façade installation, the steel elements for the building's roof top, the elevator tower, the tip and loggia roof were assembled on the ground before being hoisted to their intended location by crane for final installation. Installation cranes were only used for the installation of the loggia roof. The height of the two main cranes increased along with the growing building. They needed to be fastened to the closed core walls at regular intervals. The storey-per-storey installation of the façade was devised to avoid these fastening points. To prevent water penetrating into the shell, the façade elements were completely sealed.

Left: final installation of the tip. The top part, with steps and night-time orientation light, was brought into position by helicopter and welded into place in vertiginous heights.

Interior
Till Briegleb

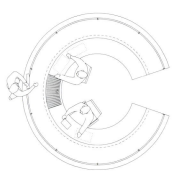

The circular reception desk (M 1:100) is equipped with all controls for the building's security and malfunction monitoring system. The vertical surfaces were clad with finely perforated aluminium panels. The horizontal surfaces, such as handbag shelf and writing surface, were covered in black leather.

In order to guarantee the well-being of a building's occupants and users, they need to be able to feel free to live and work by their own demands and requirements. This freedom can only be achieved if a building's architectural structure provides the possibility for various forms of user development. Any kind of restrictive conditions, on the other hand, lead to limitations and discontent. In a successful interior, users enjoy a high degree of flexibility and are not restricted by a domineering presence of interior design features. This is particularly true in a high-rise building, where options are inherently limited.

The façade design provided a solution for a number of problems that the occupation of a high-rise building is usually associated with. Natural ventilation, audio contact with the exterior environment and individual ventilation and lighting control are all features that would be unthinkable in a high-rise building were it not for the double-layer façade, which has enabled this office tower to achieve levels of comfort normally associated with low-level buildings. The benefits of the double-layer façade must not, however, be counteracted by an interior concept that lacks the analytical rationale and formal restraint of the exterior design concept.

Christoph Ingenhoven was determined to develop an interior design concept that centred around one of the main principles of the architectural concept: that architecture must never create the illusion of a living, functioning environment for people. 'We do not want to create vitality with this building, we want to enable it.' For the selection of materials this meant that restraint and performance were of prime importance. After all, the concept only allowed for a limited number of materials to be used throughout the building, so they could be adapted and modified according to their specific use. This restraint does not only allow the creation of an inconspicuous backdrop that fosters communication and creativity, it also corresponds to the basic idea behind the building – and Ingenhoven Overdiek und Partner other work – of regarding industrial premanufacture and modular reproduction as a fundamental principle of rational and ecological construction. The interior concept comprises the following materials: glass, perforated aluminium, high-quality plastic laminate and beech-wood for walls and ceilings and natural stone and carpet for the floors.

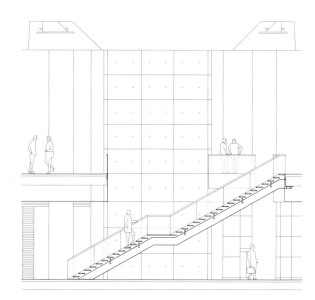

The architects were keen to avoid pretences. The building's concrete skeleton is not hidden, structural elements such as columns are finished in architectural concrete and installations and equipment are fully visible features of the interior landscape. All pre-fabricated parts are screwed, pinned, mounted flush, suspended... in short: installed at a distance to the backdrop. The interior concept attempts to avoid the illusion of homogenous white cells at all costs. Plastered walls, plaster board, wall paper or stone cladding on walls and ceilings are strictly avoided, except where unavoidable. The result is that the structure of the building is present in every room; the building's grammatical code, its structural honesty is tangible throughout the building.

The selected materials were also required to meet ecological and health standards. Any kind of infringement of the occupants' health was to be consistently ruled out and an attempt was made to calculate the energy efficiency value for each material.

The urge to avoid any pretence was extended to the finish of all materials. The natural colour and structure of the materials remain visible: the use of opaque lacquers, stains and varnishes was banned. Smooth surfaces were ruled out to retain the materials' tactile quality. Following the overall design concept, restraint was the primary concern. Where colour had to be applied, for example to plastic parts, carpets or furniture, subtle shades from the 'alpine' colour concept were chosen. The 'alpine' metaphor, rather amusing for an office tower in a completely flat part of Germany, defines a colour spectrum of limited scope and luminosity, which in turn serves to prevent garish colour highlights with which the building would dominate the occupants. The 'alpine' concept furthermore creates a strong link between the inside and outside worlds, as it was also used for the gardens and corresponds to the weather conditions usually experienced from within a high-rise building in this part of Europe. The selected colours are various shades of silver (water), white (snow), grey (stone), brown (wood), green (foliage) and blue (sky) as well as mixed shades.

The fundamental conceptual notion to create a serviceable, subtle, almost humble overall appearance for the tower meant that several materials with which large

In the waiting areas in the lobby and on level -1, long seating benches are combined with classic Le Corbusier arm chairs, both covered in black leather, complemented by glass tables for enhanced transparency. The elegant seating groups create a relaxed atmosphere of calm, suitable for all kinds of meetings and conversations.

The seating groups have been arranged in a repetetive pattern to allow proximity or distance, depending on the needs of different user groups. It is therefore possible to retreat for contemplation or, if necessary, for groups of people to communicate effortlessly.

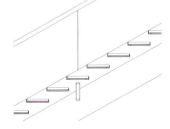

111

The garden level lounges command views into the lobby, the atria and the park: in a relaxed ambiance, one can follow the hustle and bustle inside the building or contemplate the gardens outside.

Charles Eames' Wire Chairs and Arne Jacobsen's oval table are used in the staff restaurant. The oval-shaped tables enhance communication while seating more people than circular tables. The oval tables can be placed individual or in groups. Furthermore, it is easy to place rectangular trays onto an oval table. The seat covers are a vibrant red-orange, so that the room appears lively even when it is empty (it is only used c. 2 hrs. per day).

To complement the catering service for staff members outside restaurant opening hours, several drinks and snack vending machines have been integrated into one of the foyer's walls. The vending machines have been painted in aluminium paint. The machines lack any sort of animated graphics to ensure that the restrained effect of the walls' aluminium cladding is maintained.

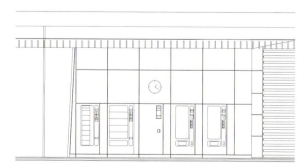

corporations tend to convey power and status were ruled out from the start; the RWE tower completely lacks bold image statements in marble, chrome or precious timber. The term with which Christoph Ingenhoven likes to describe the overall concept of the RWE HQ tower is 'softness'. How has this quality of softness been applied? Well, first and foremost, thanks to the allround glazing, yet despite the use of flint glass, a green glow permeates the entire building. This shade is picked up by the carpet and the natural stone floor: the woven carpet a relatively strong grey-green, the natural stone, a gneiss from a quarry in the Alps, a dominant grey.

Aluminium is used in perforated and non-perforated form in the façade, structural parts, furniture, the porter's console and vertical cladding; it reflects ambient colours to great effect, enhancing the harmonious colour concept. The partition walls are made of beech-wood because it has a relatively neutral colour and an even grain and because it is inexpensive and grows in Europe. The beech-wood walls are instantly recognisable as a pre-fab veneered product (again, no pretence), an effect enhanced by the perforation that dramatically improves the panels' acoustic properties. All other partition walls (with the exception of the executive floors, where they are covered in a light-grey fabric) are made of off-white high-quality laminate.

 Again, restraint was paramount, as pure brilliant white walls have a much stronger presence and are more prone to soiling. Ingenhoven Overdiek und Partner had to compromise on two points: the sanitary zones are tiled rather than clad with prefab ceramic panels, and the ceilings in the underground levels are made of plaster board – although an effective distance to the real ceil-ing could be maintained by suspending the plaster board ceilings.

Even the most consistent overall concept only works effectively if the conditions are the same throughout. But even in the special areas, where the fit-out had to comply with particular requirements, the architect's signature remains clearly visible. For the porter's console, the food distribution area, the bar and the walls of the dispensing machines – all designed by Christoph Ingenhoven – the material concept could largely be retained; in some cases it was complemented by leather surfaces.

The need to comply to a company's hierarchical structures meant that special conditions applied to the executive floors. But the architects nevertheless managed to incorporate these special features into the overall concept. The linoleum padding on the desks and tables or the separate colour identity for the cladding and carpets (green instead of blue, silvery instead of white) are perfectly integrated into the balanced emotional expression of the entire fit-out while still fulfilling the purpose of elevating the ambiance on the executive floors to a prestigious and elegant level.

The elaborate media equipment required the architects to provide additional design solutions. But even here, discretion and restraint are chosen in favour of in-your-face ostentation. The architects spent considerable time to design fold-away techniques for all technical equipment, so that video conferencing devices, overhead projectors, simultaneous translator booths and technical director booths are visible yet well integrated to reduce their spatial impact. Projection screens, table monitors, loudspeakers and security equipment are only visible when in use.

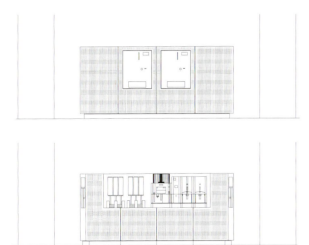

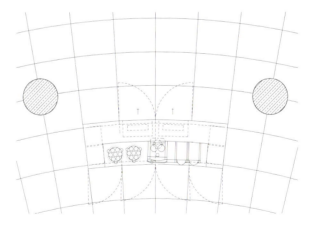

This multi-function counter, which is oriented towards the vending machine, is clad with perforated aluminium panels – just like the porter's desk, thus almost creating a product range – and the heavy-duty horizontal surface is covered in hard eloxy-coated aluminium.

During shell construction, an entire sample zone was built in order to get a comprehensive impression of space, material quality and colours. Samples of all interior elements and furniture for the conference rooms, RWE-board offices, catering rooms and sanitary zones were included in the relevant sample rooms for final specification.

Office: all final fit-out materials and details were presented together for the first time in this 'show-office', providing a preview of the ambiance to be expected in this future work place. This allowed examining and optimising planning decisions down to the minutest detail.

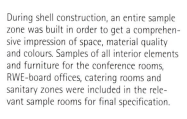

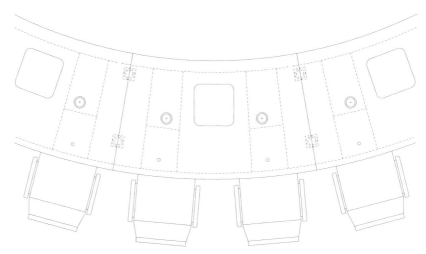

Boardroom table (M 1:30)

'It was a constant battle to make things disappear as much as possible', as Christoph Ingenhoven describes the strenuous process which was eventually concluded successfully, down to the emergency exit diagrams and the fire escape signs. Instead of opting for the usual white running man on green background Ingenhoven chose a white running man on clear background: it fulfils its purpose perfectly yet does not disrupt the harmony of the carefully designed ambiance.

Christoph Ingenhoven suffered his greatest defeat in his attempts to create maximum transparency. His repeated requests to opt for glazed partition walls, at least between the offices and the corridors, were not granted. Senior management was apparently not prepared to have their colleagues watch them at work. Christoph Ingenhoven at least managed to convince his client to accept glass elements at the top of the partition walls. But the inherent flexibility of the interior concept does, of course, allow a reversal of initial decisions: all partition walls are modular elements and can be completely dismantled – if the corporate attitude changes, so can the interior.

Christoph Ingenhoven opted not to design new furniture, although he had been granted to do so in the brief. The search for furniture that 'combines lightness and elegance with constructive ambition while conveying freedom and inconspicuousness' was bound to be more or less limited to classics. Eames, Le Corbusier and Bertoia furniture perfectly matched the formal code of the building's architecture. Colours were selected for the subtlety: black or natural leather and aluminium. An exception was made for the chairs for the cafeteria: Eames-Wire Chairs with orange fabric covers provide colour spots in a large room where people will not spend enough time to provide the colour spots themselves.

The architects advised the client in the selection of office furniture; the selected system was therefore perfectly integrated into the overall interior concept, in terms of colour (green and blue) as well as function.

In its stringency, the RWE headquarters' interior displays lightness, and in its simplicity it conveys aesthetic beauty. The cool and restrained order creates generous space. The working world inside this glass column feeds off the stimulating neutrality of the discreet backdrop.

Telephone booths with all necessary communications equipment were installed on garden level and on the 27th floor.

The boardroom table was designed in co-operation with Wilkhahn, taking the boardroom's geometry and the technical requirements into account. The aim was to devise a modular conference table system that would meet all technical requirements without compromising on aesthetics. Flat screens on electrically operated pull-outs and connections for microphones are built in flush with the table top covered in black cow leather. The vertical leg screen, clad in perforated aluminium, appears to hover in front of the table, adding to the delicate elegance of this room. All boardroom materials are taken from a building-wide selection of materials – glass and aluminium on vertical, leather on horizontal surfaces.

Hoofbeats
Lothar Baumgarten

Hoofbeats

My work for the new RWE office tower is entitled 'hoofbeats'. It is an 'in-situ' work that expresses arguments of materiality and site-specific contents. It completely blends into the architectural context and adopts the building's architectural code both in form and materials.

Through a canon derived from its stipulated manifestation, the piece endorses the set configuration of the architecture, thereby reflecting it in its own composition. In a discordant rhythm, the piece intensifies the contents of applied neologisms – terms derived from the financial pages of daily newspapers, from the language of corporate business, the capital markets and administration. They are substitutes for an accelerated language leaning towards efficiency that increasingly lacks clarity. These so-called neologisms often display a poetic and twisted comic element that frequently leads to misinterpretations as to their real meaning. In most cases they are not able to clarify a given context – on the contrary, they actually serve to confuse. They appear raw and terse or display a cynical-naive quality. They are 'signifiers' that turn into rigid sculptures resembling the stones one chewes when reading. They are ephemeral and cannot be found in the dictionary. Their inherent 'aroma' of sound and content is always a product of its time and reveals a great deal of that particular era.

This is a critical location-specific discourse that in its realisation deals with the region as its central issue. 'Hoofbeats' – grey like basalt, echoing the hard sound of forged iron on cobblestones, with silvery shiny letters like wet stones in the sunlight.

Fired enamel on raw concrete is the connection, the materials that coincide in the building's lobby, consolidating the aforementioned expressions in their own language.

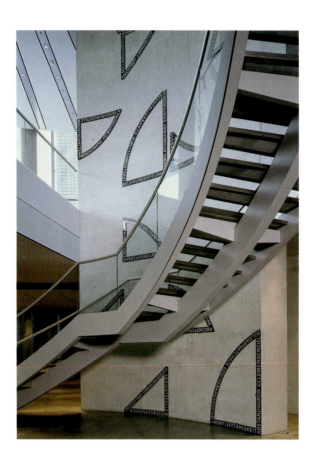

The enamelled metal strips pick up the shape of the shuttering panels of the architectural concrete walls, thus reflecting the building's grammatical code.

Above: The original art concept is based on two artists engaged in a critical dialogue with the building. The Kunstkreis (responsible for placing art in the building) has therefore decided to invite Lothar Baumgarten to contribute a piece for the lobby and to include a piece by Richard Long in the parks and gardens.
Right: The transparency and three-dimensional aspect of the open-plan lobby allow Lothar Baumgarten's work to be viewed from the outside as well as from garden level.

Neandertal Line
Richard Long

I first heard about the RWE building from Konrad Fischer, my friend and dealer in Düsseldorf, who recommended it as as good situation to make a work. So my 'Neandertal Line' is partly dedicated to Konrad, who died in 1997.

Almost all my work, whether placed outdoors or indoors, is a dialogue with a particular place, but in this unique case my stone line surprisingly came first, before the site for it at the RWE building was ceated.

It is by pure chance that the quarry at Neandertal was both a place to find local stones, (my normal practice), but also a famous place, redolent of the history of early man. (Stone Age man meets late Stone Age artists....)

Occasionally in my walking art works have used historical places as symbollic starting or ending places for walks. For example, I have started two walks from Stonehenge, in 1972 and 1999.

I made a walk in 1979, 'Windmill Hill to Coalbrookdale', which started from the place in Southern England where fields were first cleared from the forest, thus marking the birth of pastoral culture. It ended at Ironbridge, the birthplace of the Industrial Revolution.

I like the idea that 'Neandertal Line' contains both its own geologic time, it has a connection with human history, but is also a work of modern art made in 1999.

As Richard Long's piece will not be completed until the end of 1999, it appeared appropriate to show one of his earlier pieces, the 'Neandertal Line'. This piece was shown at the Kunstsammlung NRW, a regional art collection, in the spring of 1994.

NOTES FOR NEANDERTAL LINE
AND THE LANDSCAPING OF THE PARK

HOWEVER THE 'HILLS' AND 'VALLEY' ARE CONTOURED,
IT IS IMPORTANT AND NECESSARY THAT THE 'PLACE OF THE LINE'
IS FLAT AND LEVEL (BUT NOT HORIZONTAL — IT SHOULD BE
SLIGHTLY SLOPING DOWN TOWARDS THE 'LAKE')

I.E. LONGITUDIANAL SECTION:

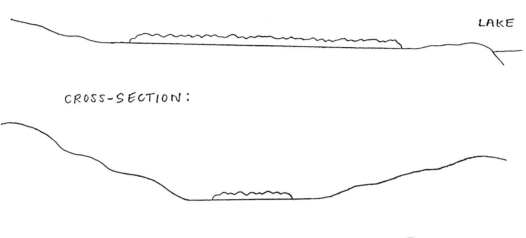

DUISBURG 1997

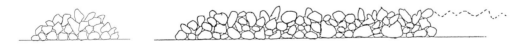

While Lothar Baumgarten's work, fitted to the lobby's architectural concrete walls, deals with the building's historical and structural roots, Richard Long's work makes a strong reference to his previous work, the 'Neandertal Line'.

Richard Long's piece is a trace of broken stone pieces, its length approximately the same as the tower's diameter; the stone trace makes an allusion to the tower's centre point and to the lake's geometry. It points into the depths of the park, therefore creating a link between the building, the landscape and space.

The sketch shows the intended effect of the c. 32-metre long 'trace of stones'. The exact position of the trace of stones and its integration into the landscape concept were discussed at length and on site with Richard Long on several occasions, and finally agreed. Fine adjustments were made on site under the architects' supervision.

Design
Achim Nagel

The erection of a modern building is today no longer a process where craftsmanship and manual production methods are combined to complete the task. Even if we should want it to be so, there would not be sufficient specialist craftsman capacities for these kind of projects, and the wages for these craftsmen would be astronomical.

Therefore, modern buildings – and high-rises in particular – should be constructed with modular elements.

Only meticulous planning of these elements as well as close quality control at manufacturing stage will ensure the quality of execution that manual craftsmanship used to, but can no longer provide.

On the strength of this argument it would appear sensible to reduce the share of shell construction in the building process as the last remaining more or less manual part. Today, shell construction accounts for around 20 - 25% of total building costs as opposed to 30 - 40% ten years ago.

Modern façades are particularly important as far as a swift and economical building process is concerned. Today, they are no longer manufactured and fitted in monolithic form but made as a system of elements that can be quickly mounted on the shell.

The development of the basic RWE tower façade element, involving numerous 1:1 test models, led to a modular serial production system. The optimised high-quality façade modules are delivered complete with sunlight protectors, glazing, fire proofing, cladding, etc., safeguarded from the shell construction process above with a special casing and then fixed to the shell. This enabled the contractors to begin with the installation of technical equipment and with the interior fit-out very soon after the shell had been completed and its scaffolding removed.

In order to accelerate the building process even further, we developed systems for a trouble-free and rapid fit-out, based on the production of factory-tested components.

Detail of the so-called fish mouth, with its built-in capacity to accommodate technical and fit-out components, and individual components of the double-layer façade where they meet the fish mouth. Thanks to the fish mouth, the structurally required construction of the concrete ceiling, with cavity floor and carpet fitted to its upper side and drop ceiling, including technical installations and anti-glare screen, fitted to its underside, could be reduced in thickness towards the glass façade to a mere 13 cm; therefore, as the photo on the right illustrates, the façade appears 100% glazed.

The precursor of the final ceiling system was the so-called 'surfboard' (left) which already contained all the features and components of the final system except for the finned cooling surface with slats.

Christoph Ingenhoven's initial sketch for the 'surfboard' concept.

We have, for example, developed a ceiling system comprising the following components:

Transverse beam
The transverse beam is fixed to the shell and is horizontally and vertically adjustable. The transverse beam construction comprises pre-installation facilities for technical equipment and is the supporting framework for the ceiling components.

Technical duct
The central technical duct accommodates all technical equipment installed during the fit-out stage. Apart form housing additional components such as lighting, cooling elements, air vents, sprinklers, fire alarms, loudspeakers, filters, etc. the modular duct allows the future integration of further technical equipment. At the same time, the technical duct determines the order of technical planning within the overall integrated planning process.

Metal cladding
The perforated metal cladding can be fitted shortly before the occupation of the offices; they define the external appearance of the ceiling.

Left: The extent of the perforation was determined by the cooling system hidden above and by the necessity for convectiveness permeating through the ceiling panels. Below: The façade as it appears during the day with and at night without lighting.

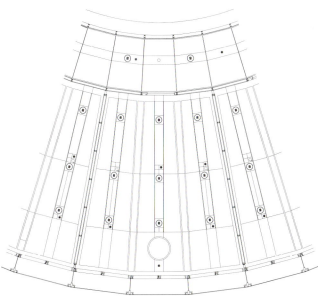

Ceiling system, typical floor (M 1:120)

The ceiling element's functionality was examined in several tests at ROM, Hamburg, and TKT-Krantz, Bergisch-Gladbach, where simulations regarding the joint effects of cooling, ventilation, fire detection and sprinkler operation were also conducted. The photo on the left shows the air speed sensors. On the right: a smoke test to examine vorticity.

Apart from optimising all technical components we integrated control panels into the partition walls next to every office door in order to achieve maximum individual flexibility in controlling the technical equipment. Similar to the ceiling element, the control panel clearly displays the controls for all technical functions in a modular structure.

Apart from room-conditioning façade functions such as a warning signal for closing the windows and various options for sun screens, anti-glare devices and lighting, other special functions such as motion detectors, call buttons, access control, etc. can also be integrated.

We continued to develop the idea of the control panel with Siemens, resulting in a mass-produced control panel that is universally deployable; the panel is EIB-compatible and can be used via switches, infrared, computer and phone; it is fully integrated into the building's technical system.

In co-operation with Siemens the architects developed a control panel for the individual control and adjustment of all office functions (light, air etc.); this control panel was finally developed into a product ready for mass-production (right). For the process of product development the material characteristics of the aluminium surfaces, multi functionality aspects and user-friendliness were examined (see photos p. 123).

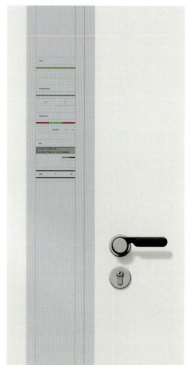

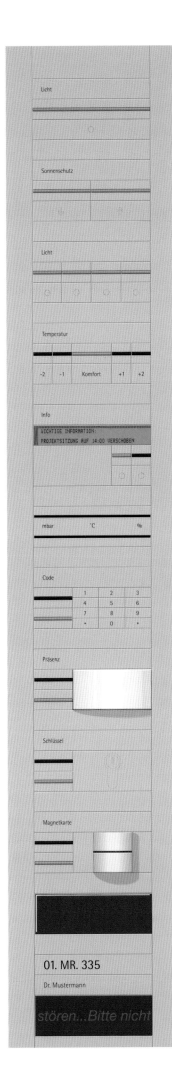

The illustration shows the control panel with all function modules

The one-button control unit with multi-colour LED status display is the new series' standard module. It covers several basic functions such as lighting, light settings (i.e. users' pre-set light preferences), service calls or displaying the message 'occupied'.

The two-button unit with two multi-colour LED displays operates two separate light settings (on/off + dimmer) and electric devices such as sun blinds, projection screens etc.

The four-button unit can control four light settings, operate the dimmer for two light groups and operate two electrical devices. The unit has one LED status and command display for each of these functions.

The 'Temperature' module enables the user to determine the desired temperature in the office by +/- 2°. The 'comfort' button activates various pre-programmed air conditioning system settings.

The 'Info' module features a two-line LCD display informing the user about office or ambient climate data. The user operates the LCD display via two buttons, one to change the display and one to switch it off.

The multi-sensor module measures air temperature, humidity and pressure and displays the relevant data which are automatically relayed to the building's central computer.

The 'Code' module features a key pad for accessing and modifying security-relevant data or to restrict the use of certain functions to a particular user group.

The 'Presence' module features a super-sensitive detector element which activates and deactivates functions such as light or air conditioning when someone enters or leaves the room. It can also be used for security purposes.

The 'Key' module has the same functions as the 'Code' module but uses a key switch in the place of a key pad.

The 'Swipecard' module features a swipecard reader for access control and electronic data processing, time-keeping, etc.

All functions of the control panels can be remotely operated. The infra-red module reads and decodes the remote control unit's commands.

The room/office ID-panel features a strip displaying room number and name of occupant as well as an LED-moving-text display for information. This panel is usually fitted in the corridors just outside each room/office, but it can also be fitted near intermediate doors or as part of this control panel.

The control panel can be installed in a variety of locations. The flexible technical duct allows hassle-free subsequent installation of new wiring and function modules should the need arise.

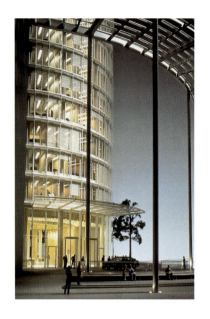

The canopy of the loggia roof is made of fish-belly shaped aluminium panels with integrated mono-crystalline photovoltaic cells facing a south-westerly direction. These cells convert solar energy into direct current that is fed into the building's grid, via change-over switch, as alternating current. We therefore have a product that not only looks good but can be used productively in other projects as well.

We have also developed solutions for interior and design issues that we have, in the meantime, modified and applied to other projects (see chapter 'Interior'). In this way, product development based on a carefully developed aesthetic language can be used to find solutions for a particular type of frequently occurring design problem.

Apart from this integrated system solution we have developed a stele product range – for certain technical functions such as time measurement, access control and intercoms – that even allows the independent arrangement of various attributes often known only at the last minute.

The forecourt is covered by a steel-frame loggia roof with integrated fish-belly slats.

Poly-crystalline cells have been built into the upper surface of the south-westerly facing photovoltaic slats; they store solar energy which is fed into the building's grid via a switch unit.

User
Dieter Schweer

A defining change

According to Christoph Ingenhoven, architect of the RWE headquarters, '...simple buildings are organised along simple and logical rules and are therefore immediately and unambiguously comprehensible'.

How true. Upon approaching the tower its structure is clearly visible; entrance zone, office floors, technical zone, executive floors and the virtually free-standing elevator tower can be instantly recognised. The whole ensemble is uncluttered and restrained, a simple cylinder allowing a full view into the offices, a transparent and open building.

The Germans' love for anglicisms led the people of the region to call the building the 'power tower'. But they also found a suitable description for it in their own language, sometimes referring to it as 'the glass giant'. This rather catchy phrase became the title of a book published on the occasion of the company's centenary. The RWE wants to be as immediately and unambiguously comprehensible to the public as its new headquarters. Not remote, closed-off and secretive as in times gone by, but modern, diverse and transparent. Like the tower.

The fact that the corporation is using the tower to demonstrate its new openness is not a contrived, hypocritical sham. With the move to the new HQ, RWE is initiating a new type of integrated communications strategy, with the aim of making the company more transparent, and abandoning the culture of seclusion in favour of a culture of dialogue. The strategy includes a new in-house magazine called 'agenda', a new image campaign and sponsoring deals. And, again, the tower.

Initially, RWE's commitment to the location 'Germany' was initially quite vague: 'We're moving house, we're not moving abroad' was the publicity campaign slogan running in the regional papers, providing information on the company. But the response was overwhelming. Thousands of people used the opportunity to visit the tower and to gather information on RWE Holding and its subsidiaries, and their activities. Families came and guided tours for architectural and engineering students were organised. A visit to the tower always included many ways in which the company presented itself and offered the chance of dialogue with the public. Due to this successful campaign 50,000 people visited the tower in the first two years after RWE moved in.

The astounded visitors realised that the corporation was serious about its dialogue approach, that it presented figures, data and facts and was open to questions and criticism. They walked through the building with growing interest, noticing how it was not at all cold, as most had expected, but decorated in warm and agreeable colours and shades.

Already during the planning and construction phase, and particularly after completion, many reviews of the new RWE tower appeared in the national and international architectural press.

The RWE tower as an example for ecological building, German Greenpeace magazine, May 1997.

The clear and logical concept has contributed substantially to the tower's success. The fine technological detailing and subtle grace not only convinced architectural critics but also visitors and occupants, even though the latter already had to adapt quite considerably to the unusual shape of the offices: they are all located towards the outside of the cylinder and are thus wedge-shaped.

Even beyond the RWE campaign, the tower was an instant hit with the people of North-Rhine-Westphalia. The main part of the tower is 120 metres high, surpassed by the elevator shaft and topped by an antenna, making the tower, at 162 metres, the highest building in the region. The tower does not appear alien or overpowering in its setting of narrow streets with predominantly two or three storey buildings – in fact, despite its weight of 35,000 tonnes it manages to appear light, friendly and inviting. RWE have been wise in extending this appearance into a real gesture of openness towards their new neighbours. Hundreds of visitors came to enjoy the view from the viewing platform. In the beginning there were so many visitors that written applications had to be made to avoid long queues, but they were always rewarded with the spectacular view from the roof of the new RWE-headquarter over the City of Essen and the region beyond.

The public accepted the tower from the word go as the City of Essen's new trademark, visible form afar, from wherever the city is approached, from the hills in the south or the motorways from all other directions – it is the first visible sign of Essen city centre, much more than merely another high-rise in the city's silhouette. No longer is the city dominated by the Gothic cathedral or, heaven forbid, a coal mine tower – the high-tech glass cylinder has become the new symbol for the Ruhr metropolis Essen.

Even athletes have endorsed the tower as a sporting challenge: every year they run the stair marathon with joyful abandon. 629 steps from the lobby to the rooftop viewing platform; the record is three and a half minutes. Even planes appear to use the tower as a landmark, as they never seem to divert very far from their landing course of 325 degrees.

The Rempen & Partner advertising agency have developed a series of billboard ads and information brochures for RWE in which the building is used to symbolise the company's re-invention.

With the construction of their new corporate headquarters at this location RWE have also consolidated their strong links to the city of Essen and the entire Ruhr region. The posters prepare the company and outsiders for the move, documenting the people of the Ruhr region in typical situations.

The loggia roof, fitted with solar cells, can be seen from the foyer of the conference zone. This is why an information panel has been installed in the foyer displaying data on the current energy generation rate and the total amount of energy generated so far.

A total success, then. Alas, there is more to the tower than meets the eye. A detailed look reveals stepping stones and edges – well, it is a 51-corner-polygone, after all. The tower's spatial concept is based on this formula: of all even shapes with the same circumference the circle has the highest surface content, i.e. the cylinder's ratio of external surface: spatial volume is better than in all other shapes. All calculations for aero-dynamics, energy requirements, impact of daylight and surface configuration are based on that formula. From the outset the principal aim was to design an ecological high-rise building, although – contradicto in adjecto – 'high-rise' and 'ecological' exclude one an-other, as conventional opinion would have us believe. Sceptics will say that in a glass tower it would be impossible to open the windows in high altitudes because of the wind, so full-time climate control would have to be installed; as there is no natural shade the windows would have to be darkened and the offices lit artificially. But of course the artificial climate would consume vast amounts of energy and have a paralysing effect on the occupants – a phenomenon experts call the 'sick building syndrome'.

In response, architect Christoph Ingenhoven has developed a façade with a second external layer and the so-called 'fish-mouth' openings between the two layers. This solution, a novelty when the RWE tower was built and meanwhile recognised as cutting-edge technology, allowed him to construct a building in which RWE staff can open the windows, work with natural daylight and be aware of the distant urban noises from below; oh, and energy consumption has been reduced by 30%. Of course, you need air conditioning some of the time.

But at least the building manages to generate some of the electricity it requires with solar energy. A closer look at the loggia roof linking the two wing buildings and covering the lobby entrance reveals photovoltaic cells integrated in the roof structure. The occupants are informed about the current rate of electricity generated by the 336 solar modules on a display in the conference zone; it also displays the total number of kilowatt hours generated so far. This may be a mere ecological gesture, but it does act as a subtle reminder to the RWE board that a corporation like the RWE 'takes its ecological responsibilities seriously'.

For Christoph Ingenhoven, the double-layer façade represents 'a defining change in high-rise building, which was hitherto dominated by the American principle of using air conditioning to create a strict separation of interior and outside environment'.

The 50-cm wide space between the façade's two glass shells is divided into climate chambers that are each as high as a full storey and as wide as the window axis. Via the 'fish mouth' – a set of slat-shaped, staggered openings – fresh outside air is drawn from below and stale, warm air from above is extracted: effectively, the building is shrouded in an insulating layer filled with perpetually renewed air. The façade is therefore virtually a realisation of Le Corbusier's notion of the breathing wall, 'le mur respirant'.

The beauty of it is that the high-tech system of the façade remains practically invisible, the eye only sees the diaphanous, translucent shell. Thanks to the air-insulation, features like mirror glass or tinted glass are not required, the view onto and into the building is unobstructed.

Visitors to the new building were given smiley-stickers in the shape of the building's plan.

The second layer lends the building a mysterious, silky shine. Looking into the building, it is as though all activity inside takes place behind a cinema screen. The effect is repeated in the opposite direction: looking out from the corridors onto the elevator shaft, the window turns into a viewing box: Essen from above. The fact that the inside windows in the offices can be opened to a 13-cm wide gap eliminates the separation from outside and inside. Via a control panel the occupants can regulate the condition in their offices: elaborate technology allows individual settings for lighting, exposure to daylight and temperature as well as other functions.

The storeys are all structured in the same manner right up to the executive floors. Access is organised via the external elevators with a short access passage leading to a circular corridor; the offices are located on the periphery of the cylinder. An elliptical conference room, toilets, kitchenette, copy and file storage rooms and service shafts are located on every floor within the cylinder core. The offices are not very deep (i.e. the distance from window to door is not excessive) and daylight reaches the corridor via skylights.

The windows stretch from floor to ceiling to make maximum use of daylight and solar heat. The angle of incoming sunlight is enlarged by sloping ceilings. The furnishing is elegant and high-quality, the desks are custom-made and even the office chairs and visitor's chairs were modified to RWE's requirements.

The formal precision is convincing. The materials used – aluminium, concrete, gneiss, wood and glass – a part of a carefully devised interior concept. The little details confirm the architect's confidence in taste and elegance: the façade element fittings, door handles, electrical sockets, mixer tabs in the washrooms, the Vitra chairs in the Casino or the Le Corbusier chairs in the lobby: nothing is vulgar, everything is functional.

The board room on the 30th floor is simply breathtaking. 36 leather Eames chairs are neatly positioned around the table with 18 recessed built-in screens. The room is covered by a slightly vaulted glass roof, allowing an unrestricted view towards the sky. Still further above is the light dome that shines like a halo during the night.

'The move to our new headquarters is also a departure' as RWE chairman Dr. Dietmar Kuhnt announced before the imminent relocation exercise. Indeed, the move by RWE Holding from its subsidiary RWE Energie's building into their own tower had more than symbolic power, as the holding company moved into a position where it was much more exposed. The distance between the 'Wattican', as the former headquarter of the Rhine-Westphalia-Electricity works were called, and the new Power Tower may not be great, but the move represents a substantial change in the company's identity: by commissioning and moving into the tower, the company has made a statement that goes beyond architectural achievement.

Technical Data

RWE AG Essen HQ office tower

Location
Opernplatz 1, Essen, Germany
opposite the Alvar Aalto theatre

Construction
June 1991 The jury decides
Late 1992 Ratification Plan B for the 'Stern' service industry centre
August 1992 Architect's contract signed
Sept. 1993 Plan B becomes legally binding
Beginning 01.07.1994
Completion 31.12.1996
Final inspection 13.03 1997

Project data
Height of the building
120 m façade
127 m elevator tower
162 m to aerial tip

Storey heights
3.00 m storage
3.75 m garden level
9.00 m lobby
3.60 m offices
3.80 m non-typical use / Board
8.00 m technical installations

Loggia roof, height
25 m to top surface photovoltaic slats

Number of storeys
2 technical installations floors + storage
1 garden-level floor
31 floors above ground level, incl.
2 technical installations floors
1 roof garden

Surface area
Building: c. 860 m^2
Parks and gardens: c. 4,800 m^2

Diameter office tower
31 m inner façade
32 m outer façade

Gross plan surface area
c. 25,200 m^2 tower
c.   4,800 m^2 parks and gardens
c.   6,000 m^2 technical installations, storage
c. 36,000 m^2 total

User surface areas
c. 12,000 m^2 offices
c.   600 m^2 conference rooms
c.   3,400 m^2 restaurants
c.   4000 m^2 other uses
c. 20,000 m^2 total

Gross spatial volume
c. 102,000 m^2 tower
c. 25,000 m^2 garden level-floor
c. 20,000 m^2 technical installations, storage
c. 147,000 m^2 total

Façade surface areas
c.   7,500 m^2 inner façade
c. 11,500 m^2 outer façade
c.   3,800 m^2 elevator tower
c.   1,400 m^2 garden level
c. 24,200 m^2 total

Space between two façade layers
0.5 m wide, with walk-on platforms, sealed between each room / office unit

Weight
50,000 t   tower's own weight

Work places
c. 500 total
c. 22 per typical floor

Staff restaurant
c. 150 seats

Elevators
4 elevators, capacity: 1,000 kg/13 persons, speed 3.5 m/s
2 glass elevators, capacity: 630 kg/8 persons, speed 0.6 m/s
2 fire brigade/goods elevators, capacity: 650/2000 kg, 8/26 persons, speed 3.5/2 m/s
1 goods elevator, capacity: 1,600 kg/21 persons, speed 0.5 m/s

Photovoltaic slats
c. 360 m^2 photovoltaic slats integrated in loggia roof

Team

Architects
Ingenhoven Overdiek und Partner, Düsseldorf
Christoph Ingenhoven, Achim Nagel, Klaus Frankenheim,
Klaus J. Osterburg, Harald Benini, Martin Slawik,
Peter Jan van Ouwerkerk, Elisabeth Vieira,
Sabine Begemann, Claudia de Bruyn, Jan Dvorak,
Michael Feist, Jürgen Gendriesch, Ulf Große, Imre Halmai,
Uwe Jürgensen, Ulrich Kluth, Ingo Kraft, Jochen Müller,
Wolfgang Nimptsch, Frank Reineke, Martin Röhrig,
Sakine Sahinbas, Norbert Siepmann, Regina Wuff

Christoph Ingenhoven, Roger Baumgarten,
Arnd Gatermann, Rudolf Rüßmann, Martin Leffers,
Michael Paprotny (competition/design & planning stage)

Despite the hectic schedule in the office, the architects' team nonetheless found the time to go on two separate sailing trips on the Ijselmeer in Holland to recharge the batteries and strengthen the team spirit.

Expert planners

Planning, load-bearing structure
Hochtief AG, Hauptniederlassung Rhein-Ruhr,
Hochtief- und Ingenieurbau, Essen; Günter Strootmann
Büro Happold Consulting Engineers Ltd., Bath/Düsseldorf
Prof. Sir Ted Happold (†), Michael Dickson, Dr. Michael Cook,
Rüdiger Lutz, Andy Dunford (competition)

Technical equipment
HL-Technik AG Beratende Ingenieure, Munich/Düsseldorf
Prof. Klaus Daniels, Dieter Henze, Dieter Leipoldt
IGK Ingeniergemeinschaft Kruck, Mühlheim/Ruhr
Dr. Bernd Schulitz, Günter Hirsch

Büro Happold Consulting Engineers Ltd., Bath/Düsseldorf
Tony McLaughlin, Gavin Thompson, Ken Carmichael

Façades
Josef Gartner & Co. Werkstätten für Stahl- und
Metallkonstruktion, Gundelfingen
Dr. Fritz Gartner, Dr. Winfried Heusler, Josef Sing

Lighting
HL-Technik AG Lichtplanung, Munich
Ulrich Werning, Clemens Tropp

Parks and gardens
Ingenhoven Overdiek und Partner, Düsseldorf
Christoph Ingenhoven, Achim Nagel, Klaus Frankenheim,
Jan Dvorak
in co-operation with WKM Landschaftsarchitekten
Weber Klein Maas, Meerbusch
Klaus Klein

Kitchen planning
Flügel Großkücheneinrichtung, Essen
Dietrich Flügel

Wind tunnel examinations
Institut für Industrieaerodynamik, Aachen
Prof. Hans-Jürgen Gerhardt

Ventilation investigation and report
HL-Technik AG Beratende Ingenieure, Munich
Dr. Jochen Stoll, Alexander Schröter

Helipad consultants
Gunter Carloff, National Border Police Chief Inspector,
St. Augustin

Structural physics
Trümper & Overath, Bergisch-Gladbach
Günter Trümper

Fire protection
Institut für konstruktiven Ingenieurbau, Wuppertal
Prof. Dr. Ing. Wolfram Klingsch

Environmental consultants
Geocontrol Umwelttechnische Beratung, Essen
Dr. Christine Prange

Soil investigations and reports
ELE Erdbaulabor, Essen
Dr. Dietmar Placzek

Quantity surveyors
Ingenieurbüro Klein, Essen
Hans-Peter Klein, Manfred Beckmann

Art consultants
Vinzentz Art in Architecture, Düsseldorf
Susanne Baronin Freytag von Loringhoven, Katharina May
in co-operation with RWE AG Essen, Dr. Gudrun Jansen

Project team at RWE AG
Prof. Dr. Ulrich Büdenbender, Dr. Hans-Peter Keitel,
Dr. Herbert Krämer, Dr. Wolfgang Ziemann
Lothar Gräfingholt, Reinhold Ziemer, Herbert Rüdelstein,
Bernhard Kellersmann, Jürgen Rath, Ulrich Greiwe, Peter
Olschewski, Uwe Brückner

Project co-ordination on behalf of the user/occupier
Lahmeyer International GmbH, Frankfurt a. Main
Heiko Borchardt, Bernd Dile, Reiner Oepen, Beatrice
Schmidt

Occupant/User
RWE AG Essen

Client/Developer
Hochtief Projektentwicklung GmbH & Co
DLZ Stern oHG, Essen
Dieter Majewski, Hasan Yüksel, Lutz Weber, Franz Klug,
Georg Schewior, Ralf Heckmann, Matthias Hundgeburth

Site management
Developer
Hochtief AG, Niederlassung Essen
Alfred Pieper, Lars Leitner, Sigurd von Bartenwerffer,
Sonja-Katharina Krüger, Harald Benini, Jürgen Reusch

Contractors

Developer
Hochtief AG, Essen office

Façades, steel structures
Josef Gartner & Co. Werkstätten für Stahl- und Metallkonstruktion, Gundelfingen

Glass
Vegla Vereinigte Glaswerke GmbH, Aachen

Air conditioning, heating, sanitary
ROM Technik für Mensch und Umwelt, Düsseldorf

Lighting
Siemens AG, Beleuchtungstechnik, Trauntreut

Electrical installations
Working group Siemens AG, Essen office & Rheinelektra, Essen office

Elevators
Thyssen Aufzüge GmbH, Essen office
and Ginsheim factory

Metal ceilings, cladding
Schmid Montage, Simmerberg/Allgäu

Natural stone
Graziano Cancian Natursteinwerk, Mönchengladbach

Solar blinds
Solonia Sonnenschutz GmbH, Langenselbold

Photovoltaics
Gesellschaft für angewandte Solarenergie ASE, Munich

Floors
Carpet Concept, Bielefeld
Buschmann KG, Duisburg

Partition walls
Intek Gesellschaft für moderne Innenbautechnik mbH, Oberriexingen

Steel stairs, bannisters
Hark Treppen, Herford

Kitchen equipment
Flügel Großkücheneinrichtungen, Essen

Parks and gardens
Schröder Garten- und Landschaftsbau GmbH, Essen

Furniture
bene Deutschland GmbH, Düsseldorf
geneal Möbelwerk GmbH & Co. KG., Essen
Knoll International, Murr
Roethlisberger AG, CH-Gümmelingen
Vitra GmbH, Weil am Rhein
Wilkhahn GmbH & Co., Bad Münder

Acknowledgements

Many people have contributed to the successful completion of the RWE project and of this book. I am profoundly grateful to all of them:
Achim Nagel, first and foremost, not only but particularly for his indefatigable support – last man standing – Klaus Frankenheim and Klaus Osterburg, as they helped steer the project away from a very bendy and bumpy road onto an almost straight and smooth path, Elisabeth Vieira, Martin Slawik and Peter Jan van Ouwerkerk, who have been instrumental in this navigation, Claudia de Bruyn, who mediated tirelessly between the client and me, Arndt Gatermann und Roger Baumgarten, who were there from the start, Bob Gansfort, without whom the project would never have existed, Imre Halmai, Michael Feist, Ulf Große, Ulrich Kluth, Jürgen Gendriesch, Frank Reineke, Regina Wulff, Martin Röhrig, Norbert Siepmann, Jan Dvorak, Sakine Sahinbas, Jochen Müller and Sabine Begemann, who worked, often night and day, to help complete this project, Dr. Friedhelm Gieske and Dr. Dietmar Kuhnt, the most generous client an architect could hope for, Dr. Hans-Peter Keitel, Dr. Herbert Krämer, Wolfgang Ziemann and Prof. Ulrich Büdenbender, the most generous and loyal client committee one could wish for, Lothar Gräfingholt, the only one who was there from beginning to end and who became a friend, Reinhard Ziemer, who was always by his side, Ilona Moos and Herbert Rüdelstein, who have welcomed 50,000 visitors to date and who have been lovely to every one of them, Heiko Borchardt and Bernd Dik, who arbitrated the most explosive argument on patient paper, Thomas Franke, who led the hysterical architect through the planning permission jungle with lots of good advice and help, Georg Temme, who came to the rescue when the proverbial hit the fan, Ted Happold, Michael Dickson and Tony McLaughlin, whom we have grown very fond of and who have taught us German architects a bit of British engineering, Dr. Siegfried Liphardt and Günter Strootmann, who helped us salvage the concept when things got really desperate, Klaus Daniels and Dieter Henze, without whose support we would still associated a boiler with the term 'technical installations', Friedel Abel, a loyal friend, Dieter Majewski, who always fulfilled his difficult role with such diplomacy, Dr. Arnold Schink and Hasan Yüksel, who never lost sight of the overall aims even when not always seeing eye to eye, Alfred Pieper, Lars Leitner, Sigurd von Bartenwerfer, Sonja-Katharina Krüger and Jürgen Reusch, who today bear no signs of problems we heaped upon them, Harald Benini, who minimised these problems considerably without ever compromising his loyalty, Fritz Gartner, Winfried Heussler, Josef Sing and Armin Schwab, without whom many things wouldn't have turned out right, and without whom the façade would have never seen the light of day, Till Briegleb, who kept a steady course, even when the book project seemed in danger, Jan Esche, for his angelic patience and much more, Petra Pieres, best boy, Michael Reiß, for the texts and more, Dr. Ulrich Schmidt and Ulrike Ruh, who expertly managed the editorial process of this book under the usual (and unusual) strains and conditions, Beate Tebartz and Stephanie Westmeyer, who produced brilliant graphics under even more strenuous conditions, Holger Knauf and Hans Georg Esch, whose photos are so effective and are looked at much more frequently than the building itself, Peter Krämer, whom I picked up from the Lufthansa inflight magazine and who made the fish belly what it is, Klaus Klein, Ulrich Werning, Clemens Tropp, Lothar Baumgarten, Richard Long, Dieter Schweer, Ulrich Behr and Joachim Stoll, whose contributions have been so successful in making often complex and important information understandable and whose often underrated contributions helped the project to succeed, Sandy Copeman and all Amalgamis for the most beautiful models I have ever seen, my friend and partner Jürgen Overdiek, who is always there when you need him and last but not least my wife Regina, an incorruptible critic of my work who never tires of emphasising the important things in life and architecture, and all the many others who have helped inventing, planning, granting building permission for, building, documenting and publishing the project.

Christoph Ingenhoven
Düsseldorf, im November 1999

Illustrations

Amalgam Modelmakers, Bristol
p. 90 (10), 92, 93

Lothar Baumgarten
p. 116 (bottom right)

Graziano Canzian, Mönchengladbach
p. 106 (9)

Michael Dannenmann
p. 136

Hans Georg Esch, Köln
p. 9, 11, 13, 17, 19, 50 (left), 63 (above left), 65, 124 (centre left), 129, 131, 137

Andreas Fechner, Wesel
p. 111 (above right), 112 (above left), 117, 128 (3), 134 (bottom left)

Konrad Fischer, Düsseldorf
p. 119

Josef Gartner & Co.
p. 68 (bottom right), 71 (22), 84 (bottom centre)

Steffen Hauser, Greenpeace
p. 108 (bottom right)

Hubert Harst, Witten
p. 56 (3: above left, centre, centre right), 57, 59 (bottom centre), 102, 103 (left), 105 (9), 109(3)

Hochtief Hauptverwaltung
p. 58 (centre), 59 (bottom left), 97 (above right), 103 (right), 104 (4), 105 (above left), 107 (bottom), 106 (top line centre), 109 (3)

Damian Heinisch, Essen
S 49 (2: above left, centre left), p. 58 (top line second from left), 62 (2), 86 (3: above left, above centre bottom right), 109 (bottom right), 110, 111 (5), 112 (5), 113 (bottom left), 115 (2: centre left, bottom right)

Bernd Hoff / Panama, Düsseldorf
p. 127

IFI, Institut für Aerodynamik, Aachen
p. 80 (2: bottom centre, bottom right)

Yasuhiro Ishimoto
p. 97 (in: Arata Isozaki, Katsura: Raum und Form, Stuttgart; Zürich: Belser, 1967: p.74/75)

Christoph Ingenhoven, sketches
p. 5, 20, 22, 24, 49, 55, 58 (3), 59 (2), 72, 95, 96, 97, 98 (2), 121

Helmut Jacoby, Halle
p. 15 (7), 28 (centre above)

Holger Knauf, Düsseldorf
p. 20 (2: bottom right, bottom right), 21 (bottom right), 29 (above left), 30/31, 32 (3), 34 (2), 35 (2), 36 (3), 37, 38 (4), 39, 40/41, 41 (2: bottom), 42 (3), 43 (4), 44 (3), 45 (2: above, bottom right), 46 (2), 47 (4), 48 (2), 49 (2: centre right, bottom right), 50 (right), 51, 52 (2), 53 (2: above left, centre left), 59 (9), 64 (3: left), 67 (bottom right), 69 (centre right), 72 (5), 73 (2: above right, bottom), 80 (above right), 81 (2), 82 (bottom right), 83, 84 (left), 86 (2: bottom centre, above right), 87 (6), 88 (4), 89 (5), 91 (3), 94 (11), 95 (6), 98 (5), 100 (4), 101 (above right), 108 (2: centre right, centre bottom right), 109 (4), 113 (above right), 114 (18), 115 (above right), 116 (2: above left, above right), 120 (bottom right), 121 (4), 122 (3), 123 (2), 124 (3: above left, bottom centre, bottom left), 125, 137, 140

Peter Krämer, Düsseldorf
p. 63 (centre), 64 (above right), 120 (o.), 121 (above left), 124 (2: above right, centre right)

Landesvermessungsamt NRW
p. 11 (Orthobild 1:5000, 1997:08:07, 4508/13)

Richard Long
p. 118 (in: Richard Long, Kunstsammlung Nordrhein-Westfalen, Düsseldorf, Richard Long, Düsseldorf, 1994), 119

Marion Nickig, Essen
p. 99 (6), 100

Eamonn O'Mahony, London
p. 45 (bottom left), 58 (above left)

RWE
p. 59 (2: bottom right), 109 (6), 127 (3), 128 (Sticker)

Christian Richters, Münster
p. 63 (centre above left)

ROM Rudolf Otto Meyer, Hamburg
p. 121 (bottom centre)

TKT Kranz, Bergisch-Galdbach
p. 75 (2), 121 (bottom right)

Weber Klein Maas, Meerbusch
p. 99 (2)

Peter Wels, Hamburg
p. 28

Jens Willebrand, Köln
p. 60, 61 (2), 82 (left), 99, 100 (3), 101 (2)

Title pages
p. 126: L'ARCA, 03/1994, Intelligente Glasfassaden, 1995, Wettbewerbe aktuell, 09/1991, AIT, 12/1996, Agenda, 01/1997, Detail, 04.05.1997, Der Gläserne Riese, 1998, L'Industria delle Costruzioni, 06/1998, Greenpeace-Magazin, 05/1997

p. 128: Baukultur, 02/1997, Fassade, 04/1995, Wila, 1997, Essener Revue, 01/1997, Hochtief, 1994, Design & Licht, 06/1997

Rempen & Partner
p. 127 (12)

Bibliography

Papers

Wettbewerbe Aktuell, 09/1991
AW – Architektur + Wettbewerbe, 06/1992
Architektur + Wirtschaft, 1993
DBZ, 10/1994
AIT, 10/1994
Bauwelt, 08.07.1994
Fassade, 04/1995
Building Design, 09/1995
Architectural Record, 10/1995
bauzentrum, 04/1996
Pace-Interior Architecture, 05/1996
Glas, 08/1996
Architectuur & Bouwen, 10/1996
Bauwelt, 22.11.1996
Intelligente Architektur, 12/1996
Architektur Magazin, 01/1997
Agenda, 01/1997
Drabert Online, 02/1997
Baukultur, 02/1997
Frankfurter Rundschau, 13.03.1997
Häuser, 03/1997
Leonardo Online, 03/1997
db, 04/1997
Wettbewerbe Aktuell, 04/1997
Neue Zürcher Zeitung, 04.04.1997
Arch+, 04/1997
Welt am Sonntag, 20.04.1997
Frankfurter Allgemeine Zeitung, 24.04.1997
Building Design, 25.04.1997
Glas, 04/1997
World Architecture, 04/1997
VFA-Profil, 04/1997
The architects' journal, 15.05.1997
Baumeister, 05/1997
Architektura Murator, 05/1997
Netscape, 05/1997
Die Welt, 31.05.1997
Green Peace, 06/1997
INTEC, 06/1997
Architectural Record, 06/1997
Architectural Review, 06/1997
Design & Licht, 06/1997
DBZ, 08/1997
Die Zeit, 22.08.1997
Frankfurter Allgemeine Zeitung, 01.09.1997
VfA Profil, 12/1997
Bauen, Wohnen und mehr, München 1998
VfA Profil, 03/1998
Architektura, 11/1998
Frankfurter Rundschau, 27.03.1999
AIT-Skript, 05/1999
ZEIT-Punkte, 06/1999
World Architecture, 07/08/ 1999
World Architecture, 09/1999

Films

Hochtief: Vom DLZ Stern zur Passarea

ROM: Bauvorhaben DLZ-Stern in Essen

WDR: 'Linie K', 27.05.1993

DW-Deutsche Welle: Wirtschaftsmagazin 'made in germany', 27.11.1997

DW-Deutsche Welle: 'Kunst & Co.', 16.09.1998

WDR: 'Kulturszene: Architektur in Düsseldorf', 14.03.1999

SR-Südwest: 'Deutsche Architektur zum Ende des Jahrhunderts', 19.07.1999

Books

Compagno, Andrea, Intelligente Glasfassaden, Zürich: Artemis, 1995

Daniels, Klaus, Technologie des ökologischen Bauens, Basel: Birkhäuser, 1995

Krichbaum, Jörg (Hg.), Internationales Architektur-Forum Dessau, Köln: Arcum, 1995

Behling, Sophia und Stefan, Sol Power. Die Evolution der solaren Architektur, München: Prestel, 1996

Herzog, Thomas (Hg.), Solar Energy in Architecture and Urban Planning, München: Prestel, 1996

Feireiss, Kirstin; Commerell, Hans-Jürgen (Hg.), Evolution Ökologie – Architektur, Berlin: Aedes, 1996

International Architecture Yearbook No. 4, Mulgrave, Victoria / Australia: The Images Publishing Group, 1997

Ingenhoven Overdiek und Partner Architekten, Wiesbaden: Nelte, 1996

Hochhaus RWE AG Essen, Düsseldorf: o. A., 1997

Wigginton, Michael, Glas in der Architektur, Stuttgart: DVA, 1997

Institut für internationale Architektur-Dokumentation GmbH (Hg.), Glasbau Atlas, München: Edition Detail, 1998

Krehwinkel, Heinz W., Glasarchitektur. Material, Konstruktion und Detail, Basel: Birkhäuser 1998

Schweer, Dieter; Thieme, Wolf, RWE – Ein Konzern wird Transparenz. Der gläserne Riese, Wiesbaden: Gabler, 1998

Nippon Sheet Glass Co., LTD. (Hg.), Space Modulator 86, RWE, Tokyo: o. A., 1999

Norbert Streits, Burkhard Remmers, Matthias Pietzcker, Reimer Grundmann (Hg.), Arbeitswelten im Wandel - fit für die Zukunft?, Stuttgart: Deutsche Verlagsanstalt, 1999

Authors

Lothar Baumgarten, born in Rheinsberg and raised in Cologne; academic studies in Cologne, Karlsruhe and Düsseldorf; he prefers to work on site, i.e. within the context of place and architecture; since 1994 he is a professor at the Hochschule der Bildenden Künste (art school) in Berlin. Exhibitions worldwide.

Uli Behr, born 1952, engineer; since 1986 director of the façade department at Josef Gartner GmbH & Co KG, Gundelfingen. Lecturer at the Munich polytechnic.

Werner Blaser, born 1924, lives in Basel where he is active as architect, designer and publicist.

Till Briegleb, born 1962, studies politics and German studies; 1991-96 cultural editor at the 'taz' daily newspaper, Berlin, since 1997 cultural editor at 'Die Woche' weekly newspaper, Hamburg; several publications on architecture, art and theatre.

Michael Dickson, born 1944, BA MSc Eng., founding partner and president of Happold practice, Bath, UK. Member of the Institute of Structural Engineers and of the Royal Society of Arts; professor at the Bath School of Architecture and Civil Engineering.

Klaus Frankenheim, born 1951, engineer; architecture degree at Düsseldorf, Cologne and Bremen; project director at Ingenhoven Overdiek und Partner, Düsseldorf.

Fritz Gartner, born 1936, prof. of engineering, engineer; 1975-98 managing director of Josef Gartner GmbH & Co. KG, Gundelfingen.

Heinrich Hacke, born 1963; structural engineering degree at Bochum University; executive site manager/project co-ordination at Hochtief, Essen.

Dieter Henze, born 1948, engineer, services technology degree at the technical college Cologne; since 1997 professor at Münster technical college for building technology and technical fit-out; several publications on ecological energy-use through regenerative external energies.

Winfried Heussler, born 1955, engineer; studies mechanical engineering at Munich polytechnic; since 1998 director of aluminium technology and head clerk at Schüco International, Bielefeld.

Christoph Ingenhoven, born 1960, engineer, studied architecture at Aachen polytechnic and Düsseldorf art school.

Klaus Klein, born 1952, engineer, studied landscape architecture at Munich polytechnic-Weihenstephan; since 1992 in partnership with Roland Weber and Rolf Maas, Meerbusch.

Richard Long, born 1945; studied at West of England College of Art, Bristol and at St. Martin's School of Art, London; lives and works in Bristol; exhibitions worldwide, included in many important art collections, several awards and publications.

Tony McLaughlin, born 1952, BSc(Hons), C.Eng.; member of the Institute of Energy, of the Chartered Institute of Building Services and the American Society of Heating, Refrigeration and Air Condition Engineering; partner in the Happold practice, Bath.

Achim Nagel, born 1959, engineer, studied architecture at Hanover polytechnic; since 1993 partner at Ingenhoven Overdiek und Partner, Düsseldorf.

Martin Pawley, architecture critic, London

Dieter Schweer, born 1953, economist, journalist; studied economics and communication sciences; director of central communications, RWE AG, Essen; several published books.

Lothar Stempniewski, born 1958; prof. eng.; structural engineering degree at Dortmundt University; project manager at Hochtief, Düsseldorf; Rüsch Research Award 1991 and Prof. Dr. Fritz-Peter-Müller-Stiftung award.

Joachim Stoll, born 1955; prof. eng.; engineer; mechanical engineer for energy and power plant technology; since 1992 director of thermal structural physics/structural climatics at HL-Technik AG, Munich.

Clemens Tropp, born 1962; engineer; studied electrical engineering with emphasis on lighting at Darmstadt polytechnic; since 1998 in partnership with Ulrich Werning, Feldafing.

Ulrich Werning, born 1942; since 1998 partnership with Clemens Tropp, Feldafing; several publications and lectures on natural daylight and artificial light.

Klaus-Dieter Weiß, born 1951, engineer; studied architecture at Munich and Aachen polytechnics; free-lance author and publisher, Minden; architectural critic for several dailies and specialist publications; several books published.